DIVINE MASTERPIECE

COLBIY LYSGRAM

TABLE OF CONTENTS

INTRODUCTION

"From the beginning, God created mankind with a unique purpose: to live in fellowship with Him, reflect His glory, and steward the earth. Yet the story of humanity took a turn when sin came in through Adam causing separation from God. But even in our brokenness, His love for us never wavered.

In a world filled with questions about identity, purpose, and clarity. It is easy to feel lost. Perhaps you have wondered why you were created or if your life is significant in God's grand design. The truth is, you were not made by chance. You are designed for glory - a life designed for God's love, purpose, and power.

In this book, we will explore God's original plan for mankind, the enduring power of His love, and how His redemptive work through Christ invites us back into a relationship with Him. We will uncover what it means to embrace this design, not just as an abstract idea, but as a life-changing reality. If you are seeking a clearer understanding of your identity in Christ, a renewed sense of purpose, or simply a deeper connection with God, this book is for you. Let's journey together to discover what it truly means to be designed for glory.

CHAPTER 1

Understanding God's Original Plan For Humanity

So God created man in His image; in the image of God, He created him; male and female, He created them. (Genesis 1:27, NKJV)

God is a God of purpose—He does everything with intention. Just as He created the sun to give light by day and the moon to shine by night, He created you and me for a purpose—His original plan for humanity.

From the very first chapter of the Bible, we are introduced to a profound truth: humanity is no accident. We were formed with intention, bearing the image of God Himself. This truth, found in Genesis 1:27, is more than a theological statement; it is the foundation of our identity, purpose, and worth.

But what does it truly mean to be created in God's image and according to His purpose? Is it merely about physical appearance, or is there something deeper? Let's explore this together.

Being made in God's image sets us apart from all other creation. It signifies our unique ability to think, reason, and create. We are capable of reflecting His attributes—love, justice, mercy, creativity, and holiness. More importantly, it affirms that we were designed to live in relationship with Him.

God's image in us is like a mirror, created to reflect His glory into the world. Though sin has distorted that reflection, His purpose for us remains unchanged. You are not an accident, nor are you merely the product of random chance. You are the intentional design of a loving Creator!

God's Original Plan for Humanity

When God created Adam and Eve, He assigned each of them a unique role. These roles reveal His original intentions for humanity.

• FELLOWSHIP:

God didn't create mankind just to exist—He created us to know Him. Fellowship is at the very heart of God's purpose for humanity. It is not an afterthought but the core of His design, reflecting His deep desire for a loving relationship with us.

God did not create us out of necessity but out of love—a love so profound that it overflows into His creation. Even now, His desire is for you to live in communion with Him. Through Christ, we are invited back into that relationship, reminding us that our greatest purpose is to know Him and to be known by Him.

In the Garden of Eden, Adam and Eve walked with God in unbroken communion, enjoying His presence daily. Genesis 3:8 offers a glimpse of this closeness: "And they heard the sound of the Lord God walking in the garden in the cool of the day" (NKJV). This simple yet profound moment reveals that fellowship with God was meant to be an integral part of their lives. It wasn't merely about worshiping Him from a distance—it was about dwelling in His presence, knowing Him, and being fully known.

This intimate relationship was not founded on fear or obligation but on love and trust. Adam and Eve were created in God's image (Genesis 1:27), uniquely designed to reflect His glory and share in His divine nature. Their fellowship with Him brought joy, purpose, and a deep sense of belonging that nothing else could provide.

However, when sin entered the world through disobedience, the bond between God and humanity was shattered. Adam and Eve, now ashamed of their sin, hid from God (Genesis 3:10). This separation was not God's doing but the result of their choice to prioritize their desires over His will. Yet, even in the face of betrayal, God's love remained unwavering.

Throughout the Bible, we see God taking the initiative to restore fellowship with His people. He walked with Enoch (Genesis 5:24), established a covenant with Abraham (Genesis 17:7), and dwelt among His people in the Tabernacle and later in the temple (Exodus 25:8). Each of these acts reveals His unwavering desire for relationship.

Ultimately, God sent His Son, Jesus Christ, to reconcile humanity to Himself. Through His sacrifice, the barrier of sin was removed, inviting us back into fellowship with God. As Paul writes, "God was in Christ reconciling the world to Himself, not imputing their trespasses to them" (2 Corinthians 5:19, NKJV).

For believers, fellowship with God is both a privilege and a calling. It is not reserved for a select few but is available to all who come to Him through faith in Christ. This relationship is deeply personal, as Jesus affirms in John 17:3: "And this is eternal life, that they may know You, the only true God, and Jesus Christ whom You have sent" (NKJV).

Fellowship with God transforms every aspect of our lives. It grants us peace amid chaos, guidance in uncertainty, and strength in weakness. It also fills us with joy, as Psalm 16:11 declares: "In Your presence is fullness of joy; at Your right hand are pleasures forevermore" (NKJV).

- **HOW TO CULTIVATE FELLOWSHIP WITH GOD**

Though fellowship with God is a gift, it requires intentional effort on our part. Just as relationships with people grow through time and dedication, our relationship with God deepens when we prioritize Him in our daily lives.

Prayer: Prayer is the lifeline of fellowship with God. It is more than just presenting requests—it is about listening to His voice and aligning our hearts with His will. As Jesus said, "But you, when you pray, go into your room, and when you have shut your door, pray to your Father who is in the secret place" (Matthew 6:6, NKJV).

Scripture: The Bible is God's primary way of speaking to us. Through its pages, we discover His character, His promises, and His plans for our lives. Regularly meditating on His Word keeps us rooted in Him. Psalm 1:2-3 reminds us that those who delight in God's law are like trees planted by streams of water, bearing fruit in every season.

Worship: Worship is more than just singing songs—it is a lifestyle of honoring God through our thoughts, words, and actions. When we cultivate a heart of gratitude and adoration, we draw closer to Him. Jesus told the Samaritan woman, "But the hour is coming, and now is, when the true worshipers will worship the Father in spirit and truth" (John 4:23, NKJV).

Obedience: Fellowship with God flourishes when we walk in obedience to His commands. Obedience is not about earning His love but about demonstrating our love for Him. As Jesus said, "If you love Me, keep My commandments" (John 14:15, NKJV).

Community: While personal fellowship with God is essential, gathering with other believers is equally important. Within a community, we encourage one another, share burdens, and grow together in faith. Hebrews 10:24-25 urges us to "consider one another to stir up love and good works, not forsaking the assembling of ourselves together" (NKJV).

• STEWARDSHIP:

As God's image-bearers, humanity was entrusted with the care of creation. Adam and Eve were given the responsibility to tend and keep the garden, reflecting God's care and provision. To this day, we are called to be stewards of the gifts, resources, and opportunities He has placed in our hands.

Stewardship is a divine calling given to humanity from the very beginning. It is not merely about managing resources but about reflecting God's character through our care, responsibility, and accountability for all that He has entrusted to us. This mandate reveals God's trust in humanity and His desire for us to participate in His work on earth.

As stewards, we are called to nurture and protect creation, ensuring its flourishing for generations to come. This responsibility remains relevant today. The way we treat the environment, use our resources, and care for others reflects our understanding of this divine mandate. In Genesis 2:15, God placed Adam in the Garden of Eden "to tend and keep it" (NKJV). This command was more than a mere task—it was an invitation to partner with God in sustaining and nurturing creation. Adam was not just a laborer; he was a steward, entrusted with the responsibility to oversee and cultivate what God had made. Stewardship also reflects the image of God within us. As bearers of His image (Genesis 1:26-27), we are called to emulate His creativity, care, and provision. Just as God provided for creation with abundance and order, we are to mirror His character by managing resources wisely and compassionately.

True stewardship extends beyond material possessions. It encompasses every aspect of our lives—our time, talents, relationships, and even the environment. Recognizing the full scope of stewardship allows us to see its relevance in both the everyday and the extraordinary moments of life.

Stewardship of the Earth:

God's command to "have dominion" over the earth (Genesis 1:28, NKJV) does not God does not grant humanity the right to exploit the earth but calls us to care for it responsibly. This responsibility includes nurturing the environment, protecting wildlife, and implementing sustainable practices that ensure future generations can thrive.

Psalm 24:1 reminds us, "The earth is the Lord's, and all its fullness, the world and those who dwell therein" (NKJV). Recognizing that the earth belongs to God should inspire us to treat it with reverence and care, honoring His creation through our actions.

Stewardship of Time:

Time is one of the most precious gifts God has given us. Each day presents an opportunity to serve Him, grow in faith, and positively impact others. Ephesians 5:15-16 urges us to "walk circumspectly, not as fools but as wise, redeeming the time, because the days are evil" (NKJV).

Being good stewards of our time means prioritizing what truly matters—our relationship with God, our families, our callings, and acts of service. It requires setting aside distractions and intentionally aligning our daily activities with God's purposes.

Stewardship of Talents and Gifts:

God has blessed each person with unique abilities and spiritual gifts. These talents are not meant to be hoarded or left unused but are entrusted to us for His glory and the benefit of others. In the Parable of the Talents (Matthew 25:14-30), Jesus emphasizes the importance of faithfully utilizing what we have been given. Those who invest their talents are rewarded, while the one who buries his talent is rebuked.

Paul reinforces this truth in 1 Corinthians 12:7, stating, "But the manifestation of the Spirit is given to each one for the profit of all" (NKJV). True stewardship means recognizing that our gifts originate from God and intentionally using them to advance His kingdom.

• STEWARDSHIP OF RELATIONSHIPS:

Relationships are a vital part of our stewardship. As parents, spouses, friends, and mentors, we are called to nurture and invest in the lives of others. Loving our neighbors as ourselves (Mark 12:31) and bearing one another's burdens (Galatians 6:2) demonstrate our commitment to stewarding relationships with care and intentionality. Strong, Christ-centered relationships reflect God's love and contribute to the spiritual growth of both ourselves and those around us.

Stewardship of Finances:

The Bible frequently addresses the responsibility of managing finances wisely. Proverbs 3:9-10 instructs, "Honor the Lord with your possessions, and with the firstfruits of all your increase" (NKJV). This stewardship includes tithing, giving generously, and exercising financial wisdom by avoiding greed and wastefulness. When we handle our resources in a way that honors God, we acknowledge Him as the true provider and demonstrate trust in His provision.

Challenges in Stewardship

Although stewardship is a divine calling, it comes with challenges. In a world driven by consumerism and self-interest, it is easy to lose sight of God's purposes. Poor management, greed, and neglect can hinder our ability to steward well, leading to missed opportunities to honor God with our resources.

Overcoming these obstacles requires humility, accountability, and a heart aligned with God's will. Through regular self-reflection and prayer, we can identify areas where we need growth and seek God's wisdom to steward our gifts, relationships, and resources more faithfully.

- **STEPS TO FAITHFUL STEWARDSHIP**

Acknowledge God as the Owner: Recognize that everything you have belongs to God. Viewing yourself as a steward rather than an owner shifts your mindset from possession to responsibility.

Pray for Wisdom: Seek God's guidance in managing your resources, time, and talents effectively. James 1:5 assures us that He grants wisdom to those who ask.

Set Priorities: Align your activities and decisions with God's purposes, focusing on what has eternal significance rather than temporary gain.

Be Generous: Freely share your blessings, whether through financial giving, acts of kindness, or investing in relationships. Generosity reflects God's heart and deepens our fellowship with Him.

Practice Accountability: Surround yourself with trusted mentors or peers who can offer counsel and encouragement, helping you remain faithful in your stewardship.

Ultimately, stewardship is an act of worship. When we faithfully manage what God has entrusted to us, we honor Him and reflect His character to the world. Colossians 3:23-24 reminds us: "And whatever you do, do it heartily, as to the Lord and not to men, knowing that from the Lord you will receive the reward of the inheritance; for you serve the Lord Christ" (NKJV).

God's call to stewardship is both a privilege and a responsibility. By embracing this divine mandate, we actively participate in His work, embody His love, and fulfill our purpose as His image-bearers. Let us steward well, knowing that our faithfulness brings glory to the One who has entrusted us with His creation and gifts.

- **DOMINION:**

God granted humanity dominion over the earth—not as a license for exploitation, but as a call to rule with wisdom, compassion, and justice. This authority is rooted in our identity as His representatives, tasked with reflecting His character in how we lead and care for His creation.

True dominion is not about dominance but stewardship—leadership that mirrors God's selflessness, justice, and compassion. When God entrusted Adam and Eve with dominion over the earth, He was not merely granting them authority; He was inviting them to reflect His character in how they governed and nurtured creation. This divine mandate carries profound responsibilities, requiring wisdom, humility, and a steadfast commitment to honoring God in all things.

Understanding Dominion in Scripture

Genesis 1:28 records God's command: "Then God blessed them, and God said to them, 'Be fruitful and multiply; fill the earth and subdue it; have dominion over the fish of the sea, over the birds of the air, and over every living thing that moves on the earth'" (NKJV).

The word "dominion" signifies both authority and stewardship—not exploitation or abuse. It calls for leadership and governance that reflect God's sovereignty, justice, and love. Dominion is not a license for selfish gain but a divine mandate to exercise responsible care over creation.

Dominion as a Reflection of God's Image

God's granting of dominion to humanity is deeply tied to our identity as His image-bearers (Genesis 1:26). Just as God governs the universe with wisdom, love, and justice, we are called to reflect these qualities in how we steward the earth. Dominion is not about control or exploitation but about leadership that aligns with God's character:

Compassionate Leadership: God's rulership is defined by compassion, mercy, and grace. As stewards of His creation, we are called to embody these attributes, ensuring that our actions benefit both humanity and the natural world.

Justice and Righteousness: Psalm 89:14 declares, "Righteousness and justice are the foundation of Your throne" (NKJV). True dominion requires upholding justice, protecting the vulnerable, and ensuring fairness in the distribution of resources and opportunities.

Creativity and Provision: Just as God provides abundantly for His creation, we are called to cultivate environments and systems that promote growth, sustainability, and flourishing for all.

REALMS OF DOMINION

- **REFINED VERSION:**

Dominion is not limited to ruling over animals or the environment. It extends to every sphere of influence God has entrusted to us—our families, communities, workplaces, and society at large.

1. **Dominion Over Creation**

Caring for the earth is a central aspect of our God-given dominion. This responsibility includes nurturing the environment, protecting wildlife, and using natural resources wisely. It also calls us to address pressing issues such as deforestation, pollution, and climate change, recognizing that how we treat the earth reflects our reverence for its Creator.

Psalm 8:6-8 beautifully captures this truth:

"You have made him have dominion over the works of Your hands; You have put all things under his feet, all sheep and oxen—even the beasts of the field, the birds of the air, and the fish of the sea that pass through the paths of the seas" (NKJV).

2. Dominion in Leadership

Dominion also applies to how we lead and influence others. Whether in the workplace, ministry, or family, we are called to lead with integrity and humility. Jesus exemplified this in His teachings on servant leadership, reminding us that true greatness lies in serving others (Matthew 20:25-28).

1 Peter 5:2-3 (NKJV) instructs:

"Shepherd the flock of God which is among you, serving as overseers, not by compulsion but willingly, not for dishonest gain but eagerly; nor as being lords over those entrusted to you, but being examples to the flock."

Godly leadership is not about control or power but about guiding and serving with a willing heart, setting an example for those we lead.

3. Dominion Over Sin

Through Christ, we are called to exercise dominion over sin and its influence in our lives. Romans 6:14 declares, "For sin shall not have dominion over you, for you are not under law but under grace" (NKJV). This victory is made possible through the power of the Holy Spirit, who enables us to resist temptation and walk in righteousness. 1 Corinthians 10:13 (NKJV) assures us:

"No temptation has overtaken you except such as is common to man, but God is faithful, who will not allow you to be tempted beyond what you are able, but with the temptation will also make the way of escape, that you may be able to bear it."

God provides the strength and guidance to overcome sin. As believers, we are no longer slaves to sin—we have been given dominion over it. In Christ, our victory is secure!

THE IMPACT OF SIN ON GOD'S PLAN FOR HUMANITY

When Adam and Eve disobeyed God, His image in humanity was not destroyed but marred. Sin introduced brokenness into every aspect of life—spiritually, mentally, morally, and relationally.

- **BROKEN FELLOWSHIP**

Sin's entry into the world was an act of direct defiance against God's perfect plan for humanity, bringing about profound and tragic consequences—foremost among them, a fractured relationship with the Creator. This rupture stands as one of sin's most devastating effects, influencing every aspect of human existence.

1. The Loss of Intimacy with God

Before the fall, Adam and Eve enjoyed an unbroken, intimate relationship with God, walking with Him in the cool of the day (Genesis 3:8). They lived in perfect harmony, free from fear or shame. However, sin created a vast chasm between humanity and God.

The first evidence of this broken intimacy was Adam and Eve's reaction to their disobedience—they hid from God in fear and shame (Genesis 3:10). This separation was not merely physical but spiritual, symbolizing the loss of connection with the Creator. Because God is holy and cannot coexist with sin, humanity found itself distanced from Him in a way it could not mend on its own.

2. Shame and Guilt

Sin introduced an awareness of guilt and shame that had never existed before. Adam and Eve, once naked and unashamed, suddenly felt the need to cover themselves with fig leaves (Genesis 3:7). This reflects the weight of sin on the human heart, distorting both self-perception and the understanding of God.

Shame leads to self-isolation—not only from God but also from others. This breakdown in relationships is one of sin's key consequences, resulting in fear, mistrust, and fractured connections between people.

3. Spiritual Death

God warned Adam that eating from the tree of the knowledge of good and evil would result in death (Genesis 2:17). This was not an immediate physical death but a spiritual separation from God. As Paul later explains, "For the wages of sin is death, but the gift of God is eternal life in Christ Jesus our Lord" (Romans 6:23, NKJV). Spiritual death is the most devastating consequence of sin—it severs humanity from the very source of life, leaving people in a state of spiritual darkness and separation from God's presence.

4. Alienation from God's Presence

Sin led to humanity's expulsion from the Garden of Eden (Genesis 3:23-24). This was both a physical and symbolic removal from God's immediate presence. The cherubim and flaming sword guarding the way to the Tree of Life serve as a sobering reminder that sin bars humanity from the fullness of God's presence.

This theme of alienation is echoed throughout Scripture, as sin continually separates individuals, families, and nations from God. Yet even in the midst of separation, God's desire for reconciliation remained clear—He immediately began unfolding His redemptive plan.

5. Struggles in Fellowship with Others

Sin not only fractured humanity's relationship with God but also disrupted harmony among people. The blame-shifting between Adam and Eve in Genesis 3:12-13 is a striking example of how sin fosters division. This relational discord escalated quickly, as seen in the tragic story of Cain and Abel (Genesis 4:8).

From jealousy and strife to conflict and broken relationships, the consequences of sin continue to plague human interactions, revealing how deeply it distorts our ability to love and live in unity.

6. A Groaning Creation

Sin's impact extended beyond humanity, affecting all of creation. The world, once in perfect balance, was subjected to futility and decay (Romans 8:20-22). The harmony entrusted to humanity's stewardship was disrupted, and the earth itself began to bear the scars of the fall. Natural disasters, disease, and suffering serve as enduring reminders that sin did not just corrupt the human heart—it left an imprint on creation itself.

DISTORTED STEWARDSHIP

The fall introduced greed, exploitation, and selfishness into humanity's relationship with creation. Instead of fulfilling the divine mandate to care for the earth, humanity began to misuse it for personal gain.

1. Exploitation Over Care

Sin distorted stewardship into greed, leading to the reckless exploitation of creation. Pollution, overconsumption, and environmental degradation are evidence of this corruption (Romans 8:22). Rather than preserving and nurturing the earth, humanity often prioritizes profit over responsibility, depleting resources without regard for future generations.

2. Neglect of Responsibility

Sin fosters laziness and carelessness, causing people to abandon their God-given duties. The parable of the talents (Matthew 25:14-30) warns against mismanagement and the failure to fulfill one's responsibilities. When humanity neglects its role as caretakers, both creation and society suffer the consequences.

3. Selfishness in Relationships

Stewardship extends beyond material resources—it includes relationships. However, sin turns stewardship inward, prioritizing self-interest over service, compassion, and justice. Proverbs 31:9 calls believers to "open your mouth, judge righteously, and plead the cause of the poor and needy" (NKJV). Yet, when selfishness prevails, relationships become transactional rather than sacrificial.

4. Idolatry of Creation

Instead of honoring God as the Creator, some elevate creation itself above Him. Romans 1:25 warns against this reversal: "They exchanged the truth of God for a lie and worshiped and served the creature rather than the Creator" (NKJV). Whether through materialism, environmental extremism, or the elevation of nature above divine authority, idolatry distorts the proper order of stewardship.

5. Inequity in Resource Use

Sin also corrupts the just distribution of resources, leading to economic and social disparities. Greed and injustice contradict God's call for equity and care for the poor. Scripture repeatedly emphasizes the importance of providing for those in need, ensuring that stewardship is exercised with fairness and compassion (Proverbs 14:31, James 2:15-16).

ABUSED DOMINION

Leadership, which was meant to be an act of service, became a tool for oppression. Yet, God's original intention for dominion remains unchanged—He calls us to lead with His heart. Dominion, as designed by God, was a sacred mandate for humanity to rule and care for creation with wisdom, compassion, and justice. It was never meant to be a license for exploitation or oppression. However, sin corrupted this divine responsibility, distorting dominion into an abused privilege. Rather than ruling as reflections of God's character, humanity often wields power for selfish gain, inflicting harm on creation and others.

Abused dominion is evident in the reckless exploitation of natural resources, where short-term gain is prioritized over sustainability and the well-being of future generations. The earth, entrusted to humanity as a gift, has been plundered, polluted, and mistreated—an undeniable reflection of greed triumphing over stewardship. But this abuse extends beyond the environment to relationships and societal structures, where authority is too often used to oppress and control rather than to uplift and serve.

Genesis 6 reveals a world before the flood that was filled with violence and corruption, a stark demonstration of how far humanity had strayed from God's original design for dominion. Instead of fostering harmony, people used their power to dominate others and perpetuate injustice. This pattern continues in modern times, where authority is frequently exercised without regard for human dignity and the well-being of others.

Abused dominion not only distorts creation but also alienates humanity from God. It is a rejection of the trust He placed in us to act as His representatives on earth. The misuse of power has repeatedly led to oppression, as seen in Exodus 1:13-14, where the Egyptians subjected the Israelites to bitter slavery, exploiting them for their own gain. Similarly, in 1 Kings 21, King Ahab and Queen Jezebel abused their authority to unjustly seize Naboth's vineyard, a stark example of how dominion, when misused, becomes a tool for greed and injustice.

Yet, despite humanity's failures, God's Word offers hope for restoration. Jesus, the ultimate example of righteous dominion, came not to be served, but to serve (Mark 10:45, NKJV). His life exemplifies the true purpose of power—to uplift, heal, and bring glory to God. Through His sacrifice, we are invited to realign our understanding of dominion with God's original intent.

In Christ, we are called to reclaim dominion as it was meant to be— rooted in service, love, and obedience to God's will. True dominion does not seek control but instead reflects God's justice, mercy, and compassion in every sphere of influence.

THE HOPE OF RESTORATION

The truth that we are created in God's image carries a profound message of hope. No matter how far we have fallen or how broken we may feel, the image of God within us is not lost—it can be restored. Through the sacrifice of Jesus Christ, we are offered forgiveness and reconciliation with God. Scripture affirms that those who accept Christ are made new: "Therefore, if anyone is in Christ, he is a new creation; old things have passed away; behold, all things have become new" (2 Corinthians 5:17, NKJV). This renewal restores us to the purpose God intended from the very beginning.

Despite the devastating impact of sin on humanity, the story does not end in brokenness. From the moment of the fall, God set His redemptive plan in motion to restore what was lost. His love for humanity remains unwavering, and through His grace, He offers the hope of restoration—a hope that brings healing, renewal, and reconciliation.

The first glimpse of this hope appears in Genesis 3:15, where God declares the coming of a future Redeemer who will triumph over the serpent: "And I will put enmity between you and the woman, and between your seed and her Seed; He shall bruise your head, and you shall bruise His heel" (NKJV). This prophetic promise points to Jesus Christ, whose life, death, and resurrection would restore humanity to fellowship with God.

Our identity is not defined by the fall, our failures, or the brokenness surrounding us. It is defined by the Creator who made us, who loves us, and who invites us to walk in the fullness of His original design for our lives.

REDISCOVERING GOD'S PURPOSE

Through Christ, the image of God within us is being restored. The Apostle Paul writes in Colossians 3:10, "and have put on the new man, which is renewed in knowledge after the image of Him that created him."

In Christ, we are no longer defined by the brokenness of sin. Instead, we are empowered to live as God intended, reflecting His image in every area of our lives.

In a world where identity is often shaped by societal expectations or personal achievements, it is easy to forget that our worth comes from being created in God's image. No matter what you have experienced or how far you feel from God's original design, His purpose for you remains. You were made to reflect His glory, steward His creation, and walk in fellowship with Him.

Being created in God's image is not just a theological truth—it is a call to action. It reminds us that our worth is not based on what we do but on who we are in Him. It challenges us to live with purpose, reflecting His character in all that we do.

As we continue this journey through God's design for humanity, let this chapter serve as a foundation. You were made with intention, created for relationship, and called to reflect His glory. No matter your past or present circumstances, the truth remains: you are created in His image, and your life carries eternal significance.

Being created in the image of God is not just a theological concept; it is a profound truth that should shape every aspect of our lives. When we pause to consider what it means to bear God's image, we are drawn to a place of deep reverence and awe. It reminds us that every human being is intentionally designed with value, dignity, and purpose. This understanding calls us to worship—not just in songs sung on Sunday but in the way we live, act, and honor our Creator daily. Worship is a life that reflects God's glory through our actions, thoughts, and attitudes.

Yet, as we reflect on this truth, it is important to acknowledge how sin has marred our ability to fully reflect God's image. Sin separates us from God, distorts our understanding of ourselves, and hinders our relationships with others. Perhaps you have felt this distortion—

moments when shame, fear, or insecurity made you question your worth. But the beauty of being created in God's image is that our worth is not dependent on our perfection. God's grace restores what sin has broken, and through His love, we can reclaim our identity.

This truth should also transform how we view others. Every person, regardless of their background, culture, or choices, is created in God's image. Do we treat others with the respect and compassion that this reality demands? It is easy to forget in moments of frustration or disagreement, but as image-bearers, we are called to reflect God's character by showing patience, kindness, and love. When we extend grace to others, we mirror the grace that God continually shows us.

Our identity as God's image-bearers also carries a call to stewardship. In Genesis, God entrusted humanity with dominion over the earth. This dominion is not a license for exploitation but an invitation to steward creation wisely and responsibly. Whether it is caring for the environment, using our resources with integrity, or nurturing relationships, every act of stewardship reflects our Creator's heart. Even in seemingly mundane tasks, we have the opportunity to honor God.

At times, we may struggle to fully trust God's design for our lives. Perhaps there are moments when we have wished for different abilities, appearances, or circumstances. Yet, as we grow in faith, we learn to celebrate the uniqueness with which God has crafted us.

Every talent, personality trait, and experience has a purpose in His plan. Do we trust Him enough to embrace our uniqueness and use it for His glory?

Living as an image-bearer also means finding purpose in the ordinary. Washing dishes, running errands, or sitting in silence may not feel significant, but when done with a heart of gratitude and service, even these moments can glorify God. It is a perspective shift that transforms our daily routines into acts of worship. What would happen if we approached every task with the mindset that we are reflecting God's love and faithfulness?

Community is another vital aspect of our identity. Being created in God's image reminds us that we were not meant to journey through life alone. Fellowship with other believers allows us to grow, encourage one another, and reflect God's love in tangible ways. Do we actively seek opportunities to build relationships that point us and others back to God?

This understanding also brings hope for the future. No matter the challenges we face, knowing that we are created in God's image gives us an anchor of hope—one that assures us of His love, His presence, and His promises. How does this hope inspire you to trust Him more fully, even in uncertain seasons?

As image-bearers, we are called to holiness. This is not a call to perfection in our strength but an invitation to reflect God's character through the power of His Spirit. Holiness shapes our choices, relationships, and responses to life's trials. It is a journey of surrender, allowing God to mold us into His likeness. Are there areas in your life where God is calling you to reflect His holiness more fully?

Finally, being created in God's image reminds us of our role as co-creators. Just as God is the ultimate Creator, He invites us to participate in building, innovating, and contributing to the world around us. Whether through art, teaching, parenting, or leadership, our creativity reflects His. Are there gifts or ideas you have been hesitant to pursue? Trust that God can use them in ways beyond what you imagine.

This chapter invites us to rest in the truth of who we are in Christ. We bear His name, His likeness, and His purpose. It is a call to live with intentionality, honor Him in all we do, and trust that His design for us is good. When we walk in this understanding, our lives become a reflection of His glory—a beacon of hope and love in a world that desperately needs it. both.

- **Reflection: Who Are You in God's Image?**

As you reflect on the truth that you are created in the image of God, consider how this shapes your identity and purpose. What does it mean for you to be made in His image? How can you live out the purpose He has for you?

Take a moment to ask yourself:

Do I recognize my value as a reflection of God's image, rather than basing it on what I do or how others perceive me?

How does understanding that I am created in God's image influence my worship of Him?

In what ways can I reflect His glory more intentionally—both in personal devotion and corporate worship?

How am I displaying God's nature in my relationships, creativity, and work?

Am I living out God's original intentions for me: fellowship with Him, stewardship of His creation, and exercising dominion with love and care?

Being made in God's image means I bear His name. How can I represent Him well in my speech, actions, and attitudes?

Are there areas in my life where I have fallen short in reflecting His character? How can I seek growth in those areas?

Do I regularly thank God for the gift of being created in His image?

Do I sometimes wish I were different in appearance, abilities, or personality?

How can I learn to trust and celebrate God's unique design for me?

CHAPTER 2

A Perfect Plan for The Creation

"Then God saw everything that He had made, and indeed it was very good." (Genesis 1:31, NKJV)

Genesis 1:31 stands as a triumphant declaration in the story of creation: everything God made was very good. This statement encapsulates the perfection, harmony, and divine intention behind all that exists. From the celestial bodies in the heavens to the intricate ecosystems on earth, creation bears the unmistakable fingerprints of its Creator.

At the center of this divine masterpiece is humanity—uniquely made in God's image and entrusted with the sacred responsibility of stewardship. As we explore the beauty and order of creation, we will uncover how God's love is reflected in the world around us and examine how we can faithfully fulfill our calling to care for the earth.

Creation is not just a display of divine power; it is a masterpiece—a living work of art that reveals God's wisdom, creativity, and love. From the brilliance of the stars that illuminate the night sky to the vast oceans teeming with life, the natural world testifies to a Creator who is both intentional and good. At the heart of this intricate design is humanity, set apart to nurture and steward God's creation. This chapter delves into the harmony of creation, God's purpose for mankind within it, and the practical ways we can live as faithful stewards of the earth.

The Harmony of Creation

God's Creative Order

Genesis 1 vividly depicts God's step-by-step creation of the universe, each day building upon the last to form a world perfectly designed to sustain life. Light, water, land, plants, and animals were all carefully crafted in preparation for humanity, the pinnacle of His creation.

The creation process unfolds deliberately, with each phase establishing the foundation for the next:

- Day 1 – Light and Darkness: God separated light from darkness, introducing the concept of day and night.

- Day 2 – Sky and Waters: He created the firmament to divide the waters, forming the sky.

- Day 3 – Land and Vegetation: Dry land emerged, and plant life was established to sustain future inhabitants.

- Day 4 – Celestial Bodies: The sun, moon, and stars were placed to govern time and mark the seasons.

- Day 5 – Aquatic and Avian Life: The seas and skies were filled with living creatures.

- Day 6 – Land Animals and Humanity: God created land animals and crowned His creation with humanity, made in His image.

Each step reflects the meticulous care of a Creator who designed everything to function in perfect harmony.

- **Ecosystems: A Symphony of Life**

Consider how ecosystems operate—a seamless interplay of life-sustaining systems. Forests produce oxygen, oceans regulate climate, and bees pollinate plants, ensuring food production. This intricate balance is not accidental but intentional.

- **As Psalm 19:1-2 declares:**

"The heavens declare the glory of God, and the firmament shows His handiwork. Day unto day utters speech, and night unto night reveals knowledge."

Creation itself testifies to God's wisdom, inviting us to marvel at the brilliance of His design.

- **The Role of Rest: The Sabbath in Creation**

When God created the heavens and the earth, He established a perfect balance and order in all things. From the very first moment of creation, everything He made was good. Genesis 1:31 declares, "Then God saw everything that He had made, and indeed it was very good." The phrase "very good" captures the essence of God's design—a world filled with purpose, beauty, and harmony. Every element of creation, from the vast heavens to the depths of the seas, from the towering trees to the creatures that roam the land, was intentionally crafted to fulfill a unique role in the divine order.

Humanity, created in God's image, stands as the pinnacle of His creation, entrusted with the sacred responsibility of stewardship. The harmony of creation is revealed in the interconnectedness of all things—the trees bearing fruit, the oceans sustaining life, the sun and moon marking times and seasons. Each part of creation reflects God's wisdom and creativity, and humanity was called to live in harmony with it.

Our role as stewards is to both appreciate and protect this harmony. We are charged with ensuring the flourishing of creation, recognizing that every aspect of God's world reflects His character and purpose. By caring for His creation, we honor God and fulfill His design for us as caretakers of His masterpiece.

THE GIFT OF SABBATH REST

The Sabbath was not merely a day of rest but a sacred time to reflect on, honor, and delight in the perfection of God's creation. Genesis 2:2-3 states, "And on the seventh day God ended His work which He had done, and He rested on the seventh day from all His work which He had done. Then God blessed the seventh day and sanctified it because in it He rested from all His work which God had created and made."

God did not rest because He was weary but to establish a divine pattern for humanity. The Sabbath is a gift—a time set apart for contemplation of God's goodness and rest amid our labor. It serves as a reminder of the inherent harmony in God's design, where work and rest are meant to exist in perfect balance.

Sabbath rest also reinforces a deeper truth: God is the Creator, and we are His creation. It is an opportunity to pause, realign our hearts with His purpose, and acknowledge that our well-being does not depend solely on our efforts but on His provision. Observing the Sabbath is an act of trust—recognizing that the rhythms God established are for our good.

Moreover, the Sabbath invites us to honor the very cycle of creation itself. Just as God worked for six days and rested on the seventh, we are called to partake in this divine rhythm. In a world that often glorifies constant work and productivity, the Sabbath offers a countercultural call to stop, rest, and remember that everything God made was "very good"—including us.

Through the Sabbath, we align ourselves with God's divine order and express gratitude for the gift of creation. It is a reminder that we are part of something far greater—His perfect, harmonious world—and that resting in Him is an act of faith, a declaration that His design is trustworthy and good.

The psalmist beautifully reflects on this harmony in Psalm 104:24: "O Lord, how manifold are Your works! In wisdom, You have made them all. The earth is full of Your possessions." God's wisdom is evident in the intricate balance of creation—ecosystems working in unison, seasons bringing renewal, and even the smallest creatures playing vital roles.

CREATION REFLECTS GOD'S GLORY

Every aspect of creation reveals God's greatness. Isaiah 40:26 proclaims, "Lift your eyes on high, and see who has created these things, who brings out their host by number; He calls them all by name, by the greatness of His might and the strength of His power; not one is missing." From the vast expanse of the galaxies to the finest grain of sand, creation stands as a testimony to God's infinite power and boundless creativity.

The splendor of creation vividly reflects God's majesty, wisdom, and character. Every detail of the natural world—from the towering mountains to the delicate petals of a flower—points back to the Creator. Psalm 19:1-2 declares, "The heavens declare the glory of God, and the firmament shows His handiwork. Day unto day utters speech, and night unto night reveals knowledge." Creation itself is like a silent song, ceaselessly proclaiming God's greatness to all who take the time to observe it.

The vastness of the universe speaks to God's limitless power. The stars, galaxies, and celestial bodies display the magnitude of His creative ability. Each element of creation functions in perfect harmony—planets orbit with precise balance, the sun provides light and life, and ecosystems flourish through intricate interdependence.

These reveal not only His power but also His intentionality, wisdom, and care in crafting a world where everything has a purpose.

The beauty of the earth—from cascading waterfalls to lush forests—mirrors the beauty of God Himself. Isaiah 6:3 affirms this truth: "Holy, holy, holy is the Lord of hosts; the whole earth is full of His glory!" Creation is an extension of God's holiness, reflecting His attributes in ways that can be seen, felt, and experienced.

At the pinnacle of His creation, God placed humanity—made in His image (Genesis 1:27). Our capacity for thought, creativity, and love reflects His divine nature. When we live in alignment with His purpose, we magnify the glory of God already evident in creation. Paul reminds us in 1 Corinthians 10:31, "Therefore, whether you eat or drink, or whatever you do, do all to the glory of God." Every action, when done in obedience to Him, becomes a reflection of His glory.

- **mankind's unique role**

While all of creation holds value, humanity occupies a unique and sacred position. Genesis 1:26-27 declares, "Then God said, 'Let Us make man in Our image, according to Our likeness; let them have dominion over the fish of the sea, over the birds of the air, and over the cattle, over all the earth and over every creeping thing that creeps on the earth.'" Unlike any other creature, humans were made in God's image and entrusted with a distinct purpose—one not of exploitation, but of stewardship and partnership with the Creator.

Being made in God's image is the foundation of humanity's uniqueness. This likeness does not refer to physical appearance but to attributes that mirror God's nature—our ability to reason, create, and make moral choices. Humans possess a deep moral consciousness, an inherent creativity, and the capacity for meaningful relationships, all of which reflect God's character. Ecclesiastes 3:11 affirms this distinction: "He has made everything beautiful in its time. Also, He has put eternity in their hearts." This eternal perspective, this longing for something beyond the material world, sets humanity apart from all other creation.

1. God's Love Revealed in Creation

Provision in Abundance

God, in His goodness, provides abundantly for all our needs—food, water, shelter, and even beauty. His generosity is evident in the natural world, where every resource is designed to sustain and enrich life. Acts 14:17 affirms this truth: "He did not leave Himself without witness, in that He did good, gave us rain from heaven and fruitful seasons, filling our hearts with food and gladness."

CREATION AS A REFLECTION OF GOD'S CHARACTER

Majesty: The towering mountains and vast oceans reflect His grandeur.

Attention to Detail: The intricate patterns of DNA and the delicate symmetry of a snowflake reveal His precision.

Care: The way ecosystems sustain life demonstrates His nurturing nature.

God's provision is evident in the abundance of creation. From the nourishment that sustains us to the beauty that inspires us, every detail is a testament to His love. Matthew 6:26 reminds us: "Look at the birds of the air, for they neither sow nor reap nor gather into barns; yet your heavenly Father feeds them. Are you not of more value than they?"

THE GIFT OF BEAUTY

The colors of a sunset, the fragrance of flowers, and the rhythmic crash of ocean waves—each of these is a gift designed to draw us closer to God. Romans 1:20 declares, "For since the creation of the world His invisible attributes are clearly seen, being understood by the things that are made, even His eternal power and Godhead, so that they are without excuse."

God's creation is more than just a backdrop for human life; it is a direct expression of His heart. Psalm 19:1 proclaims, "The heavens declare the glory of God, and the firmament shows His handiwork." The beauty of creation is a testament not only to God's infinite wisdom and power but also to His loving kindness toward all He has made. Each element of creation serves a purpose—whether for nourishment, shelter, or as a reflection of the Creator's magnificence.

Psalm 8:3-6 beautifully expresses this truth:

> "When I consider Your heavens, the work of Your fingers,
> The moon and the stars, which You have ordained,
> What is man that You are mindful of him,
> And the son of man that You visit him?
> For You have made him a little lower than the angels,
> And You have crowned him with glory and honor.
> You have made him to have dominion over the works of Your hands;
> You have put all things under his feet."

Just as creation bears witness to God's beauty, we, as His image-bearers, are called to reflect His glory. During His earthly ministry, Jesus reminded His followers of God's care for all creation—and how much more He cares for them. In Matthew 6:26-30, He speaks of how God provides for the birds of the air and the lilies of the field, affirming that we are of far greater value in His sight.

Creation and Relationship

Our God is relational. His relational nature is a defining characteristic of His identity, revealed consistently throughout Scripture. From the first moments of creation to His ultimate promise of eternal communion with us, God demonstrates His deep desire for connection with humanity. This truth is not only awe-inspiring but also central to understanding our purpose and relationship with Him.

Genesis 1:26-27 highlights this relational nature:

"Then God said, 'Let Us make man in Our image, according to Our likeness; let them have dominion over the fish of the sea, over the birds of the air, and over the cattle, over all the earth and over every creeping thing that creeps on the earth.' So God created man in His image; in the image of God He created him; male and female He created them."

The phrase "Let Us make man in Our image" reveals the relational nature of the Trinity. God the Father, the Son, and the Holy Spirit existed in perfect fellowship before time began. This divine relationship serves as the blueprint for human relationships—both with God and with one another.

The creation of Eve further demonstrates God's intention for humanity to live in relationship with others. In Genesis 2:18, God declares, "It is not good that man should be alone; I will make him a helper comparable to him." By creating Eve, God established the first human relationship, designed to reflect the love, unity, and cooperation found within the Trinity.

Human relationships are central to God's plan for creation. Families, friendships, and communities are meant to mirror His relational nature. Through these connections, we learn to love, serve, and grow, fulfilling God's command to "be fruitful and multiply; fill the earth and subdue it" (Genesis 1:28).

God's creation invites us into a personal relationship with Him. Everything we see in our daily lives serves as a reminder of His presence, provision, and promises. Recognizing God as relational transforms how we live. We are not merely subjects of a distant deity but cherished sons and daughters, invited into an intimate relationship with our Creator. This relationship is cultivated through prayer, worship, and immersion in His Word.

Furthermore, God's relational nature calls us to extend His love to others. Just as we are recipients of His grace, we are called to reflect His heart in our interactions with those around us—loving, forgiving, and serving as He does.

JESUS AND CREATION

Jesus Christ, the eternal Word of God, is inseparably linked to creation. He is not only the Savior who redeems but also the Creator through whom all things were made. Everything in existence—spiritual and physical, visible and invisible—was created through Christ and for His glory. He sustains all things, ensuring the harmony and order of the universe. When we recognize Jesus' role in creation, our understanding of His divinity, authority, and deep involvement in both the world and our lives is profoundly enriched. John 1:1-3 (NKJV) declares:

"In the beginning was the Word, and the Word was with God, and the Word was God. He was in the beginning with God. All things were made through Him, and without Him, nothing was made that was made."

Jesus, the Word of God, existed before time began and was actively involved in creation. He was not merely present but was the divine agent through whom God's creative power was expressed.

Throughout His earthly ministry, Jesus demonstrated His authority over creation:

Calming the Storm: In Mark 4:39 (NKJV), Jesus rebuked the wind and waves, saying, "Peace, be still!" His command over nature revealed His divine power and sovereignty.

Multiplication of Loaves and Fish: In John 6:1-14, Jesus fed thousands with only a few loaves and fish, displaying His ability to provide abundantly and miraculously.

Turning Water into Wine: In John 2:1-11, His first miracle at Cana demonstrated His power to transform the natural order.

Just as Jesus was central to the first creation, He is also the foundation of the new creation. His death and resurrection ushered in the promise of redemption and restoration.

CORINTHIANS 5:17 (NKJV) DECLARES:

"Therefore, if anyone is in Christ, he is a new creation; old things have passed away; behold, all things have become new."

Through Christ, believers are transformed, reflecting the renewal He brings to all creation. Revelation 21:5 (NKJV) affirms this hope:

"Then He who sat on the throne said, 'Behold, I make all things new.' And He said to me, 'Write, for these words are true and faithful.'"

CHALLENGES IN STEWARDING CREATION

The Fall's Impact

Before the Fall, Adam and Eve enjoyed a perfect and harmonious relationship with both God and creation. They were entrusted with the responsibility of tending and keeping the garden, reflecting their role as stewards of God's creation. Genesis 2:15 (NKJV) states:

"Then the Lord God took the man and put him in the garden of Eden to tend and keep it."

This stewardship was a divine partnership in which humanity nurtured and cared for creation without strain or resistance. However, sin disrupted this harmony, introducing toil and frustration into what was once joyful labor. Genesis 3:17-19 (NKJV) reveals the consequences of the Fall:

"Cursed is the ground for your sake; in toil, you shall eat of it all the days of your life. Both thorns and thistles it shall bring forth for you, and you shall eat the herb of the field. In the sweat of your face, you shall eat bread."

The earth, once a source of abundant provision, now resisted humanity's efforts. What was once a joyful act of stewardship became painful and arduous.

Sin not only made stewardship difficult but also corrupted humanity's relationship with creation. Instead of nurturing the earth, people began to exploit it selfishly. Greed, waste, and environmental destruction reflect the ongoing impact of sin on the way we interact with the world.

This exploitation stands in stark contrast to God's original intention for humanity—to protect and sustain creation. Proverbs 12:10 (NKJV) reminds us:

"A righteous man regards the life of his animal, but the tender mercies of the wicked are cruel."

A disregard for creation stems from a broken relationship with the Creator, leading to the misuse of resources and harm to the environment. True stewardship can only be restored when humanity returns to God's original design—one of care, respect, and responsible dominion.

Modern Challenges

In today's world, humanity faces increasingly complex challenges in caring for creation:

Pollution: Plastic waste and toxic chemicals contaminate ecosystems, harming wildlife and human health.

Deforestation: The large-scale destruction of forests leads to habitat loss, reduced biodiversity, and contributes to climate change.

Overconsumption: Excessive consumption and wasteful habits deplete natural resources and disrupt ecological balance.

Climate Change: Driven by greenhouse gas emissions and unsustainable practices, climate change poses a global threat. Rising temperatures, melting ice caps, and extreme weather events endanger lives, ecosystems, and economies.

Biodiversity Loss: Many species face extinction due to habitat destruction, poaching, and pollution, disrupting the delicate balance of creation.

Psalm 24:1 (NKJV) reminds us:

"The earth is the Lord's, and all its fullness, the world and those who dwell therein."

As stewards of God's creation, we are called to treat the earth not as a resource for reckless exploitation, but as a sacred trust. Responsible care for the environment reflects our reverence for the Creator and our commitment to His divine plan.

THE PARABLE OF THE TALENTS

In this parable, a man prepares for a journey to a distant country and entrusts his wealth to his servants. To one, he gives five talents; to another, two talents; and to the last, one talent—each according to their ability. The servants who received five and two talents invest wisely, doubling their master's wealth. However, the servant with a single talent, driven by fear, buries it in the ground, yielding no return.

When the master returns, he commends the faithful servants for their diligence and rewards them accordingly. In contrast, he rebukes the unfaithful servant for his inaction, calling him lazy and fearful.

UNDERSTANDING FROM THE PARABLE

God Entrusts Us with Resources According to Our Abilities

The master distributed talents based on each servant's ability. Likewise, God gives us unique gifts, opportunities, and responsibilities. While the amount we receive may differ, the expectation of faithfulness remains the same for all.

Romans 12:6 (NKJV): *"Having then gifts differing according to the grace that is given to us, let us use them."*

1. **Faithfulness in Small Things Leads to Greater Responsibilities**

The servants who used their talents wisely were rewarded with more. In the same way, when we are faithful with what God has given us—no matter how small—we prepare ourselves for greater opportunities in His kingdom.

Matthew 25:23 (NKJV): *"His lord said to him, 'Well done, good and faithful servant; you were faithful over a few things, I will make you ruler over many things. Enter into the joy of your lord.'"*

2. Fear and Inaction Lead to Loss

The servant who buried his talent allowed fear to dictate his actions. Instead of taking responsibility, he blamed his master's character for his failure. Fear and hesitation keep us from stepping out in faith, resulting in missed opportunities and an unfulfilled purpose.

2 Timothy 1:7 (NKJV): *"For God has not given us a spirit of fear, but of power and love and a sound mind."*

3. God Expects Us to Use What We Have Been Given

The unfaithful servant was not rebuked for having only one talent but for failing to use it. God calls us to maximize whatever He has entrusted to us—whether it be time, resources, skills, or influence. True stewardship means actively using our gifts for His glory.

James 1:22 (NKJV): *"But be doers of the word, and not hearers only, deceiving yourselves."*

4. The Consequences of Unfaithfulness

The parable ends with a solemn warning: the unfaithful servant's talent is taken away and given to the one who had ten. This illustrates an important truth—our stewardship will be judged, and unfaithfulness has lasting consequences.

Matthew 25:29-30 (NKJV):

"For to everyone who has, more will be given, and he will have abundance; but from him who does not have, even what he has will

be taken away. And cast the unprofitable servant into the outer darkness. There will be weeping and gnashing of teeth."

Application to Daily Life

1. Examine Your Gifts

What has God entrusted to you? Take time to reflect on your skills, time, resources, and opportunities. Recognizing your gifts is the first step toward using them effectively.

2. Take Action

How can you invest your talents for God's glory? Whether through service, generosity, leadership, or mentorship, seek to multiply the blessings you've received. True stewardship involves intentional and active participation.

3. Overcome Fear

Fear can paralyze and prevent you from stepping into your God-given purpose. Trust in God's guidance and strength, knowing that He empowers those who act in faith. Don't let fear hold you back from fulfilling your calling.

4. Seek Eternal Rewards

Live with the awareness that your stewardship is ultimately accountable to God. Earthly success fades, but faithfulness to His calling yields eternal rewards. Prioritize what has lasting value in God's kingdom.

CHALLENGES IN STEWARDING CREATION

The Fall and Its Consequences

When God entrusted humanity with the responsibility to steward creation, it was a divine calling rooted in harmony, care, and purpose. However, the fall of Adam and Eve introduced sin into the world, significantly disrupting humanity's ability to fulfill this role. The consequences of the Fall continue to challenge our stewardship of creation today.

1. The Curse on the Ground

One of the immediate effects of the Fall was the curse God pronounced on the ground. This curse made laborious toil a necessary part of survival and disrupted the once-harmonious relationship between humanity and the earth.

Genesis 3:17-18 (NKJV): *"Cursed is the ground for your sake; in toil, you shall eat of it all the days of your life. Both thorns and thistles it shall bring forth for you."*

What was once a fruitful and cooperative creation now resists human effort, making stewardship more challenging.

2. Broken Relationships

The Fall fractured not only humanity's relationship with God but also with creation. Instead of serving as caretakers, humanity began to see creation as something to dominate, exploit, or even battle against. This shift distorted the balance God originally intended.

Romans 8:20-21 (NKJV): *"For the creation was subjected to futility, not willingly, but because of Him who subjected it in hope; because the creation itself also will be delivered from the bondage of corruption into the glorious liberty of the children of God."*

Even creation itself groans under the weight of sin, longing for restoration and renewal.

3. Human Conflict and Mismanagement

The Fall also introduced conflict among humans, leading to disputes over land, resources, and governance. Corruption, greed, and negligence have further hindered humanity's ability to steward creation effectively.

James 4:1-2 (NKJV): *"Where do wars and fights come from among you? Do they not come from your desires for pleasure that war in your members? You lust and do not have. You murder and covet and cannot obtain. You fight and war."*

This ongoing struggle for control and power undermines collective efforts to care for the earth and its resources.

4. Environmental and Societal Impacts

The compounded effects of sin have led to global crises, including climate change, food insecurity, and the loss of biodiversity. These challenges serve as stark reminders of humanity's failure to live out God's original stewardship mandate.

Hosea 4:3 (NKJV): *"Therefore the land will mourn, and everyone who dwells there will waste away with the beasts of the field and the birds of the air; even the fish of the sea will be taken away."*

This prophetic warning paints a vivid picture of the devastating consequences of neglecting God's design for creation. However, it also serves as a call to action—a reminder that we are responsible for restoring what has been broken.

5. Practical Ways to Live as Faithful Stewards

Cultivate Awareness

Educate yourself on the impact of human activity on the environment. Awareness is the first step toward meaningful change. Stay informed about environmental challenges and the biblical foundation for stewardship.

Practice Conservation

Make intentional choices to reduce waste and protect natural resources:

Conserve water and energy by adopting sustainable habits.

Minimize the use of single-use plastics.

Support sustainable farming and ethical consumption.

Advocate for Stewardship

Encourage others to view creation care as a spiritual responsibility. Share resources, engage in discussions, and lead by example through mindful living and community initiatives.

Honor the Sabbath

Embrace rhythms of rest and renewal for both yourself and creation. Allow the land to rest by practicing sustainable agriculture, recycling resources, and respecting natural cycles. Stewardship is not just about work—it is also about recognizing the value of restoration and balance.

1. **Personal Stories of Stewardship**

Joseph: Steward of Egypt's Resources

Joseph's story is a powerful example of faithful stewardship. Betrayed by his brothers and sold into slavery, he rose to prominence in Egypt through integrity, wisdom, and God's favor. As second-in-command under Pharaoh, Joseph was entrusted with managing Egypt's resources during years of abundance and famine.

Genesis 41:39-41 (NKJV): *"Then Pharaoh said to Joseph, 'Since God has shown you all this, there is no one as discerning and wise as you. You shall be over my house, and all my people shall be ruled according to your word; only regarding the throne will I be greater than you.'"*

Through foresight and diligence, Joseph's stewardship saved countless lives. He balanced immediate needs with long-term provision, demonstrating how faith and wisdom can bring security and stability.

Lydia: Steward of Resources for God's Kingdom

Lydia, a successful merchant of purple cloth from Thyatira, exemplifies stewardship through generosity and hospitality. After her conversion, she used her wealth and influence to support the early church, offering her home as a gathering place for believers.

Acts 16:14-15 (NKJV): *"Now a certain woman named Lydia heard us. She was a seller of purple from the city of Thyatira, who worshiped God. The Lord opened her heart to heed the things spoken by Paul. And when she and her household were baptized, she begged us, saying, 'If you have judged me to be faithful to the Lord, come to my house and stay.' So she persuaded us."*

Lydia's story illustrates that stewardship extends beyond financial resources. By opening her home and using her influence, she actively contributed to the growth of the early church, reminding us that generosity is a vital aspect of faithful living.

Nehemiah: Steward of Leadership and Vision

Nehemiah, a cupbearer to King Artaxerxes, displayed exceptional stewardship in leadership. Leaving his position of comfort, he took on the task of rebuilding Jerusalem's walls, relying on prayer, strategic planning, and perseverance.

Nehemiah 2:17-18 (NKJV): *"Then I said to them, 'You see the distress that we are in, how Jerusalem lies waste, and its gates are burned with fire. Come and let us build the wall of Jerusalem, that we may no longer be a reproach.' And I told them of the hand of my God which had been good upon me, and also of the king's words* *that he had spoken to me. So they said, 'Let us rise and build.' Then they set their hands to this good work."*

Despite opposition, Nehemiah's leadership inspired others to take action. His unwavering faith and commitment to restoration highlight the importance of stewardship in leadership—demonstrating how vision, courage, and faith can bring about transformative change.

Reflection: Who Are You in God's Image?

How do you see God's love reflected in creation?

What practical steps can you take to live more sustainably and honor God's creation?

How can you instill a sense of stewardship in future generations, teaching them to value and care for God's creation?

In what ways does your stewardship reflect your trust in God's provision and guidance?

Are there areas of your life—resources, talents, or time—that you need to surrender more fully to His plan?

Like Joseph, are you prepared to use your position, wisdom, and influence to benefit others, even in difficult circumstances?

Lydia used her resources to support God's work. How can you use your home, skills, or finances to further His kingdom?

CHAPTER 3

The Fall and Its Consequences

Therefore, just as through one-man sin entered the world, and death through sin, and thus death spread to all men because all sinned."
(Romans 5:12, NKJV)

In the beginning, God created a world filled with beauty, harmony, and purpose. Humanity, formed in His image, stood as the pinnacle of creation—entrusted with dominion and designed for fellowship with Him. Yet, this perfect relationship was shattered by a single act of disobedience.

The Fall of Adam and Eve in the Garden of Eden is a story many of us know, but its significance can often feel distant—like an event from a far-off past, affecting people we struggle to relate to. However, the consequences of that moment are not confined to ancient history. They ripple through time, shaping every aspect of our lives today. The Fall was about more than just one act of disobedience; it was about a relationship that was fractured, trust that was broken, and a world that has never been the same since.

THE STORY OF ADAM AND EVE'S DISOBEDIENCE

The Garden of Eden was a paradise crafted by God, filled with everything Adam and Eve needed to flourish. At its center stood two significant trees: the Tree of Life and the Tree of the Knowledge of Good and Evil. God's command to them was clear:

"And the LORD God commanded the man, saying, 'Of every tree of the garden you may freely eat; but of the tree of the knowledge of good and evil you shall not eat, for in the day that you eat of it you shall surely die.'" (Genesis 2:16-17, NKJV)

This command was not meant to restrict but to protect. God granted Adam and Eve the freedom to enjoy all of creation while calling them to obedience and trust in His authority.

However, the serpent—a cunning manifestation of Satan—approached Eve with deceitful words, planting seeds of doubt:

"Has God indeed said, 'You shall not eat of every tree of the garden'?" (Genesis 3:1, NKJV)

By distorting God's truth, the serpent led Eve to question His goodness. Enticed by the promise of divine knowledge, she took the fruit and ate it, then gave some to Adam, who also ate. In that moment, sin entered the world, and its effects were immediate and devastating:

Shame and Guilt: They became aware of their nakedness and attempted to cover themselves with fig leaves (Genesis 3:7).

Fear: For the first time, they hid from God (Genesis 3:8-10).

Blame and Division: Adam blamed Eve, and Eve blamed the serpent, revealing how sin fractured human relationships (Genesis 3:12-13).

Pain and Hardship: Childbirth became painful for women, and labor became toilsome for men.

Separation from God: Most significantly, they were banished from Eden, losing access to the Tree of Life and the intimate fellowship they once had with God.

HOW SIN SEPARATES US FROM GOD

Sin creates a deep chasm between humanity and God—a separation that goes beyond physical distance. It disrupts the intimate relationship for which we were created, leaving a void that only He can fill. When Adam and Eve sinned in the Garden of Eden, their immediate reaction was to hide from God— a powerful illustration of what sin does: it drives us away from His presence.

God's holiness is pure and untainted, and sin, by its very nature, cannot coexist with Him. This separation is not because God withdraws from us but because sin blinds us to His presence and hardens our hearts. Isaiah 59:2 vividly describes this reality:

"But your iniquities have separated you from your God, and your sins have hidden His face from you so that He will not hear" (NKJV).

Sin builds barriers, creating a spiritual disconnect that keeps us from experiencing the fullness of His love, guidance, and peace.

This separation often manifests as guilt, shame, and spiritual emptiness. Just as Adam and Eve attempted to cover themselves with fig leaves, we try to mask our brokenness with superficial solutions. Yet nothing can truly restore what sin has severed. The story of Cain—who distanced himself even further from God after killing his brother, Abel—demonstrates how sin not only separates us from God but also distorts our relationships with others.

Yet, even in our estrangement, God longs for reconciliation. He pursues us, just as He did with Adam and Eve, asking, "Where are you?" His love is relentless, offering us a way back through repentance and the redemptive work of Jesus Christ. Romans 5:8 reminds us of this hope:

"But God demonstrates His own love toward us, in that while we were still sinners, Christ died for us" (NKJV).

Though sin separates, God's grace bridges the gap, calling us back into the relationship we were created to enjoy.

GOD'S ENDURING LOVE AND PLAN FOR REDEMPTION

The Promise of Redemption

God's love for humanity is unchanging and immeasurable. Despite Adam and Eve's disobedience and the devastating consequences of sin, His love has never wavered. Rather than abandoning humanity,

He set in motion a divine plan of redemption to restore the broken relationship. This plan stands as a testament to His enduring love and His desire to reconcile us to Himself.

When Adam and Eve sinned, it could have marked the end of God's relationship with humanity. Yet, in His mercy, He chose to extend hope rather than judgment alone. Genesis 3:15 provides the first glimpse of this hope:

"And I will put enmity between you and the woman, and between your seed and her Seed; He shall bruise your head, and you shall bruise His heel" (NKJV).

This verse, often regarded as the first proclamation of the gospel, foreshadows God's intention to send a Savior who would conquer sin and its effects.

The promise of redemption echoes throughout the Old Testament as God unfolds His plan through covenants, prophecies, and acts of deliverance. In His covenant with Abraham, He declares:

"In you, all the families of the earth shall be blessed" (Genesis 12:3, NKJV).

This blessing points to Jesus Christ, who would ultimately fulfill God's plan to redeem humanity.

The sacrifices of the Old Testament further illustrate this promise. Each offering for atonement foreshadowed the ultimate sacrifice—Jesus Christ, the Lamb of God, who takes away the sin of the world (John 1:29, NKJV). The prophets also foretold this coming redemption. Isaiah describes the suffering Servant who would bear the iniquities of many:

"He was wounded for our transgressions, He was bruised for our iniquities" **(Isaiah 53:5, NKJV).**

This promise was fulfilled in Jesus Christ. Through His life, death, and resurrection, He accomplished what humanity could not. He lived a sinless life, offering Himself as the perfect sacrifice to satisfy God's justice and reveal His boundless love. As Paul writes:

*"But God demonstrates His own love toward us, in that while we were still sinners, Christ died for us" **(Romans 5:8, NKJV).***

Yet, God's promise of redemption extends beyond individual salvation to the restoration of all creation. Paul describes this cosmic renewal in Romans 8:21:

"Because the creation itself also will be delivered from the bondage of corruption into the glorious liberty of the children of God" **(NKJV).**

God's plan encompasses not only the healing of human souls but also the renewal of His entire creation.

The promise of redemption is a call to hope. No matter the depth of our failures or the weight of our sins, God's love reaches us. He invites us to receive His grace, live as His redeemed people, and join Him in His mission to restore the world. Through Christ, the promise of Genesis is fulfilled, and humanity is restored to the purpose and fellowship for which it was created.

The Invitation to Return

Throughout Scripture, God calls humanity to repentance and restoration:

"Return to Me, and I will return to you," says the LORD of hosts. **(Malachi 3:7, NKJV).**

"Come to Me, all you who labor and are heavy laden, and I will give you rest." (Matthew 11:28, NKJV).

Reflection: Surrendering to God's Grace

Take a moment to reflect on these questions:

What does the promise of redemption in Genesis 3:15 reveal about God's character and His commitment to humanity?

How does understanding God's patience in His redemptive plan shape your perspective on trusting His timing in your own life?

When you reflect on Jesus' sacrifice as the fulfillment of God's plan, how does it personally impact you?

In what areas of your life do you struggle to fully embrace the truth of redemption and God's unconditional love?

What does it mean for you to live as someone redeemed by God's grace?

How can you reflect God's redemptive love in your relationships with others?

In what ways can you actively participate in God's broader plan for redemption within your community and beyond?

Are there specific areas in your life where you sense God inviting you to trust Him more deeply in His redemptive work?

How do passages like John 3:16 or Romans 5:8 deepen your personal understanding of God's love?

How does the promise of the renewal of all creation inspire you to live with greater hope and purpose today?

CHAPTER 4

Redeemed by His Love

"For God so loved the world that He gave His only begotten Son, that whoever believes in Him should not perish but have everlasting life."
(John 3:16, NKJV)

The story of redemption is not an afterthought in God's plan for humanity—it is the ultimate expression of His profound love. From the very beginning, God's desire was never for us to fall into sin or be separated from Him. Yet, even in the face of sin's devastating consequences, His love remained steadfast. Rather than abandoning humanity, He made a way for redemption.

God's plan, revealed throughout Scripture, finds its fulfillment in the life, death, and resurrection of Jesus Christ. His sacrifice is the bridge that restores our relationship with our Creator, offering us the hope of eternal life.

In this chapter, we will explore the depth of God's love, the cost of His sacrifice, and the transformative power of Christ's redemption.

JESUS AS THE FULFILMENT OF GOD'S REDEMPTIVE PLAN

The arrival of Jesus Christ on earth was not a coincidence but a fulfillment of divine design. In His infinite wisdom, God knew from the very beginning that humanity would need a Savior. The moment sin entered the world, He set His redemptive plan into motion.

Throughout the Old Testament, we see glimpses of Christ foreshadowed in the sacrificial system—a precursor to the ultimate sacrifice yet to come. Every offering made for atonement pointed forward to Jesus, the Lamb of God, who would take away the sins of the world.

Jesus' coming was the fulfillment of prophecy. Isaiah 53 speaks of the suffering servant who would bear the sins of many, a prophecy Jesus fulfilled through His suffering, death, and resurrection. He was more than a teacher or a prophet—He was the Son of God, sent to redeem mankind.

The significance of Jesus' role in God's redemptive plan cannot be overstated. His sinless life made Him the perfect sacrifice, wholly sufficient to cleanse us from sin. On the cross, He bore the full penalty of our transgressions, paying the price for our redemption with His own blood.

As Romans 5:8 declares, **"But God demonstrates His love toward us, in that while we were still sinners, Christ died for us"** (NKJV). His willingness to endure the suffering of the cross was not merely an act of obedience—it was the ultimate act of love, offered to every person who would ever walk the earth.

HOW CHRIST'S SACRIFICE BRIDGES THE GAP BETWEEN GOD AND MANKIND

Before the fall of Adam and Eve, humanity lived in perfect fellowship with God. Sin, however, created a vast chasm between mankind and the Creator. The consequences of sin brought spiritual death, and every person was born into this separation. Yet, through Jesus Christ, the gap between God and humanity was bridged.

Jesus' death on the cross served as the ultimate atonement for our sins. Through His sacrifice, He reconciled us to God, restoring the relationship that sin had broken. As Paul writes in 2 Corinthians 5:18, "Now all things are of God, who has reconciled us to Himself through Jesus Christ..." (NKJV).

Jesus did more than pay the price for our sins; He provided a direct way for us to approach God once again. In the Old Testament, the high priest would enter the Holy of Holies once a year to offer a sacrifice on behalf of the people—a temporary solution to the problem of sin. But when Jesus died, the veil in the temple was torn in two, signifying that through His death, direct access to God was made available to all believers.

This is why Jesus declared in John 14:6, "I am the way, the truth, and the life. No one comes to the Father except through Me" (NKJV). Through Him, we are restored to the Father and invited back into the fellowship that was once lost. The separation caused by sin has been permanently overcome.

Because of Christ's sacrifice, our relationship with God is no longer dependent on rituals, intermediaries, or the blood of animals. This profound act of love fulfilled God's promise to redeem His people. The reconciliation made possible by Jesus' death and resurrection is not merely a theological concept; it is deeply personal and transformative.

Through Jesus, salvation is freely offered as a gift—an undeniable testament to God's grace. Paul underscores this truth in Ephesians 2:8-9, "For by grace you have been saved through faith, and that not of yourselves; it is the gift of God, not of works, lest anyone should boast" (NKJV). This grace reminds us that our reconciliation with God is not earned through human effort or good deeds but is received by faith in the finished work of Christ. It is an invitation to lay down the burden of self-righteousness and rest in the sufficiency of Jesus' sacrifice.

Christ's sacrifice does more than remove the barrier of sin—it restores the intimate fellowship between God and humanity. Just as Adam and Eve once walked with God in the Garden, believers are now invited to walk with Him daily, led by His Spirit. This restored relationship is a source of guidance, strength, and comfort.

Through prayer and the indwelling of the Holy Spirit, believers experience a direct and personal connection with the Creator. As Romans 8:15-16 declares:

"For you did not receive the spirit of bondage again to fear, but you received the Spirit of adoption by whom we cry out, 'Abba, Father.' The Spirit Himself bears witness with our spirit that we are children of God" (NKJV).

The intimacy of calling God "Abba" serves as a powerful reminder of the close, familial relationship we now enjoy because of Christ.

THE ETERNAL IMPACT OF CHRIST'S SACRIFICE

The eternal impact of Christ's sacrifice is profound. It was not merely an event that occurred over two thousand years ago; it is a reality that continues to shape our lives today and into eternity. Before Jesus came, sin separated us from God. The world was filled with pain, suffering, and a deep longing for restoration. But through His death on the cross, Jesus changed everything. He made it possible for humanity to be reconciled with God in a way that was previously impossible.

When Jesus died, He didn't simply erase our past sins—He opened the door to a new way of living, one that begins the moment we believe in Him. Salvation is not just about securing a place in heaven someday; it is about experiencing a transformed life with God here and now. Through Jesus, we are no longer bound by the weight of sin. Instead, we are invited to live in freedom, purpose, and hope.

The beauty of Christ's sacrifice is that it does not only change our future—it transforms us in the present. In Ephesians 2:5-6, Paul writes, "Even when we were dead in trespasses, [God] made us alive together with Christ… and raised us up together, and made us sit together in the heavenly places in Christ Jesus" (NKJV). Jesus' sacrifice grants us a new identity—one where we are no longer defined by our past mistakes or sinful nature. We are made new. We are forgiven. And we are now empowered to live according to God's will.

Christ's death also removed the barrier between humanity and God. The moment Jesus died, the veil in the temple was torn in two (Matthew 27:51), symbolizing that we no longer need a priest to approach God on our behalf. Through Jesus, our mediator, we have direct access to the Creator of the universe. We can speak to Him, listen to Him, and experience His presence in our daily lives.

Through Jesus, we are offered eternal life—not just in the sense that we will live forever after we die, but in the sense that we can walk in a restored relationship with God starting now. John 3:16 declares, "For God so loved the world that He gave His only begotten Son, that whoever believes in Him should not perish but have everlasting life" (NKJV). This is a life that is not bound by the limitations of this world—it is a life that transcends time and space. Rooted in God's love, this eternal life begins the moment we place our trust in Jesus and continues forever.

Perhaps the most remarkable aspect of Christ's sacrifice is that it does not only transform us individually—it changes the entire world. Romans 8:21 speaks of creation itself being set free from the bondage of corruption and being restored. When Jesus returns, He will make all things new. The world as we know it—broken and imperfect—will be restored to its original beauty and purpose. Every tear will be wiped away, and there will be no more pain, suffering, or death. That is the ultimate hope of the Christian faith.

The impact of Christ's sacrifice is eternal because it changes everything—how we live, how we love, and how we see the world. It is not merely an event we remember; it is the foundation of our faith and the source of our hope. Through His sacrifice, we are offered forgiveness, a renewed relationship with God, and the promise of eternal life. That truth should radically shape the way we live each day.

THE ROLE OF THE HOLY SPIRIT IN REDEMPTION

The role of the Holy Spirit in redemption is both profound and essential. After Jesus' death and resurrection, He did not leave us to navigate life alone. Instead, He promised the Holy Spirit, who would come to empower, guide, and comfort us. The Holy Spirit plays a central role in our redemption by helping us understand what Christ has done for us, leading us into all truth, and transforming us into His image.

One of the first roles of the Holy Spirit in redemption is convicting us of our sins. Before we come to know Christ, we are often unaware of just how far we have fallen short of God's glory. The Holy Spirit works in our hearts to reveal that sin, showing us our need for a Savior. This conviction is not meant to condemn us but to draw us toward the grace and forgiveness found in Christ. Jesus said in John 16:8, "And when He has come, He will convict the world of sin, and of righteousness, and of judgment" (NKJV). Without the Holy Spirit, we would lack the awareness and desire to seek God's forgiveness.

Once we accept Christ's sacrifice and begin our journey of faith, the Holy Spirit continues His work by transforming our hearts. He indwells every believer and begins the process of sanctification, making us more like Christ. Galatians 5:22-23 describes the fruit of the Spirit—love, joy, peace, patience, kindness, goodness, faithfulness, gentleness, and self-control. These qualities are the natural outworking of the Holy Spirit's presence in our lives, evidence that we are being conformed to Christ's image. This transformation is not something we can achieve on our own—it is the work of the Holy Spirit within us.

Moreover, the Holy Spirit empowers us to live out God's will. In Acts 1:8, Jesus promised that the Spirit would empower His followers to be His witnesses—not only in words but in action. The Spirit gives us boldness, courage, and wisdom to live according to God's purposes, regardless of the challenges we face. Whether speaking truth in difficult circumstances or serving others in love, the Holy Spirit equips us to fulfill our calling and live out the redemption we have received.

Beyond empowerment, the Holy Spirit deepens our relationship with God. He is our Comforter, standing beside us in moments of doubt, fear, and pain. Romans 8:16 declares, "The Spirit Himself bears witness with our spirit that we are children of God" (NKJV). The Holy Spirit assures us that we are not abandoned, that we belong to God, and that our redemption is secure. He also intercedes for us in prayer, speaking on our behalf when we do not have the words to express our needs (Romans 8:26). This intimate connection with the Holy Spirit reminds us that God is actively involved in our lives, guiding, encouraging, and shaping us to become more like Jesus.

Ultimately, the Holy Spirit leads us into the fullness of the life that Christ offers. From the moment we place our faith in Him, the Spirit is with us—teaching, convicting, comforting, and empowering. Without the Holy Spirit, the process of redemption would be incomplete, for He is the one who brings the reality of God's grace into our daily lives. Through His presence, we are continually reminded that redemption is not just a past event but an ongoing transformation that draws us closer to God every single day.

REDEMPTION AND RESTORATION OF CREATION

Redemption and restoration go hand in hand with God's ultimate plan for humanity and the world. When we think of redemption, we often focus on what Christ accomplished on the cross—how He paid the price for our sins so that we could be reconciled to God. But redemption is not limited to humanity; it is a broader concept that encompasses all of creation. Sin did not only affect our relationship with God—it also impacted the world around us. Creation itself has been groaning under the weight of the fall, longing for the day when it will be restored to its original glory.

From the very beginning, when God created the heavens and the earth, everything was "very good" (Genesis 1:31). There was perfect harmony between humanity and creation. Adam and Eve were placed in the garden, entrusted with its care. But when sin entered the world, everything was marred—our relationship with God, our relationships with each other, and even the earth itself. Romans 8:20-22 tells us that "creation was subjected to futility" because of sin, and it eagerly awaits the day when it will be "set free from its bondage to corruption" and restored to its original purpose.

The beauty of Christ's redemption is that it is not just personal salvation—it is the promise of the ultimate restoration of all things. The Bible speaks of a time when God will make everything new, redeeming and restoring creation to its intended state. This promise is vividly portrayed in Revelation 21:1-5, where John describes a new heaven and a new earth. In this renewed world, God will dwell among His people, and there will be no more death, sorrow, or pain. What was once broken by sin will be completely renewed, and all will be made right again.

However, this process of redemption and restoration is not something that will only happen at the end of time—it has already begun. Through Jesus' work on the cross, the kingdom of God has been inaugurated. His resurrection marks the firstfruits of the new creation. 2 Corinthians 5:17 declares, "If anyone is in Christ, he is a new creation; old things have passed away; behold, all things have become new." This renewal begins with us as individuals, as we are made new in Christ—but it does not end there. It extends to the world around us.

As believers, we are called to participate in this redemptive work. We are stewards of God's creation, entrusted with its care. This means being responsible with our resources, caring for the environment, and promoting justice and peace. When we live in a way that reflects God's love for creation, we actively join in His greater work of redemption and restoration.

The redemption and restoration of creation ultimately point to the hope of a new heaven and a new earth, where God will dwell with His people and everything will be made right. It is the fulfillment of God's original plan for humanity and the world. As we wait for that day, we can be assured that redemption is already at work—both in us and in creation. The brokenness we see is not the end of the story. Through Christ, healing has begun, and one day, all things will be restored to the perfection God intended from the very beginning.

EMBRACING FORGIVENESS AND WALKING IN THE FREEDOM OF REDEMPTION

When we accept Jesus as our Lord and Savior, we are not only forgiven—we are also set free. Sin, which once held us captive, no longer has dominion over us. The forgiveness Christ offers is not merely a pardon for past mistakes; it is a transformative power that breaks the chains of sin and grants us true freedom.

In Ephesians 1:7, Paul writes, "In Him we have redemption through His blood, the forgiveness of sins, according to the riches of His grace" (NKJV). Redemption means that we have been bought back from the slavery of sin. Christ paid the ultimate price so that we might live in the fullness of His grace, no longer bound by sin's power.

However, living in the freedom of redemption does not mean living without responsibility. Jesus' sacrifice not only frees us from sin but also calls us to a life of obedience and purpose. Romans 12:1 urges us to "present [our] bodies as a living sacrifice, holy, acceptable to God, which is [our] reasonable service" (NKJV). In response to God's immense love, we are called to live in a way that honors Him.

Walking in the freedom of redemption also means walking in the power of the Holy Spirit. Jesus promised that the Holy Spirit would empower believers to live righteously (John 14:26). Through the Holy Spirit, we are equipped to follow God's will and produce fruit that reflects His work in our lives.

LIVING IN THE NEW IDENTITY

Living in our new identity in Christ is one of the most powerful aspects of the Christian life. When we accept Jesus as our Savior, we are not merely forgiven of our sins—we are given a completely new identity. This identity is rooted in who Christ is, not in who we were before we knew Him. Yet, it's easy to dwell on the past—our mistakes, our failures, or the labels that once defined us. But the truth is, in Christ, those things no longer define us.

The Bible declares that we are new creations in Christ (2 Corinthians 5:17). Our old self, with all its baggage, has been put to death, and we have been raised to new life. This transformation is not just about a fresh start—it's about an entirely new way of living. As citizens of God's kingdom, we are called to reflect His glory and fulfill His purpose. We are now sons and daughters of the Most High, adopted into God's family through Christ's redemptive work. With this new identity comes new privileges, new responsibilities, and a renewed perspective on the world.

However, embracing this new identity can sometimes feel challenging. We still live in a broken world, and struggles may tempt us to revert to old patterns of thinking and behaving. The key to living out our identity in Christ is internalizing God's truth and allowing it to shape our thoughts, actions, and decisions. We must consistently remind ourselves of what Scripture says—that we are forgiven, loved, chosen, and empowered by the Holy Spirit to walk in victory.

Living in our new identity also means embracing our God-given purpose. Our transformation is not just for ourselves—it's about being part of something greater. We are called to share God's love with others, to serve as His hands and feet in the world, and to reflect His character in all we do. This may look like extending kindness to those in need, seeking justice for the oppressed, and demonstrating integrity in every aspect of our lives. When we allow God's love to work through us, we become agents of transformation in the world around us.

It's important to acknowledge that living in our new identity does not mean we will never struggle. Temptations, difficulties, and moments of doubt will still arise. Yet, in those moments, we must cling to the truth of who we are in Christ. We don't have to rely on our strength or abilities; instead, we can lean on God's grace, trusting that He has equipped us for this new life.

Ultimately, living in our new identity is a journey. It's not about achieving perfection but about growing progressively more like Christ as we deepen our relationship with Him. And as we walk in this identity, we become a beacon of light to those around us, revealing the love and hope we have found in Jesus.

THE POWER OF THE CROSS IN DAILY LIFE

The power of the cross is more than a historical event that took place over 2,000 years ago. It is a living, transformative reality that continues to impact our daily lives. When we look at the cross, we see more than Jesus' sacrifice—we see the depth of God's love and the power to overcome sin, shame, and even death itself. But how does this power translate into our everyday lives?

One way the power of the cross affects us daily is by reminding us of God's immense love. Jesus didn't just die for humanity in general—He died for you. He knew every mistake, every flaw, and every struggle you would face, yet He still chose the cross. When we wake up each day, knowing we are loved by the Creator of the universe gives us the strength to face whatever comes our way. The cross is a constant reminder that we are never alone, and that God's love is unconditional, unshakable, and never-ending.

The cross also empowers us to live in freedom. One of its most profound truths is that it paid the price for our sins. Through Jesus' sacrifice, we are forgiven, and the chains of guilt and shame are broken. This doesn't mean we won't face challenges or make mistakes, but it does mean we no longer have to carry the burden of past sins. The power of the cross lifts the weight of regret, allowing us to walk in grace—both for ourselves and for others. When struggles arise or past mistakes haunt us, we can remind ourselves that the cross has already covered it all. As Scripture declares, "There is therefore now no condemnation for those who are in Christ Jesus" (Romans 8:1).

Another way the cross impacts our daily lives is in our relationships. The cross teaches us the power of forgiveness. Jesus didn't just offer us forgiveness—He modeled it. In our daily interactions, we are called to forgive as He has forgiven us. The power of the cross compels us to extend grace to those who hurt us and to seek reconciliation in broken relationships. Forgiveness is not always easy, but when we remember the mercy we have received, it becomes possible to extend that same mercy to others.

Living in the power of the cross also means embracing a new purpose. Jesus died to reconcile us to God, but He also calls us to be ambassadors of that reconciliation. The cross challenges us to live lives of service and love, helping others experience the same grace and freedom we have found. In our daily decisions, we are called to reflect His love in everything we do—whether that means being kind to a difficult coworker, showing patience with family, or standing up for justice when we witness wrongdoing. The cross doesn't just transform our hearts; it reshapes the way we engage with the world around us.

Finally, the power of the cross reminds us that no matter what we face, victory is already assured. The cross is the ultimate triumph over sin, death, and darkness. Life's struggles may leave us feeling defeated, but the truth remains—Jesus has already won the victory. We live in that victory, even in moments of pain or hardship. Because of the cross, we have hope for today and confidence for tomorrow, knowing that Christ has secured our eternal triumph.

In our daily lives, the power of the cross is not just a theological concept—it is a practical source of strength, guidance, and transformation. As we reflect on the cross, it empowers us to live with purpose, forgiveness, freedom, and love, showing the world the incredible difference Christ makes.

THE CALL TO SHARE THE GOOD NEWS OF REDEMPTION

The call to share the Good News of redemption is central to the Christian faith. It is an invitation for every believer to participate in God's mission to restore humanity to Himself. This call is not limited to pastors, missionaries, or those in formal ministry—it is for every follower of Christ. The world desperately needs to hear this message of hope, grace, and transformation.

At the heart of this calling is the understanding that redemption is a gift. In His infinite love and mercy, God sent His Son, Jesus, to pay the price for our sins and bridge the gap between humanity and Himself. This gift of salvation is free, but it was never meant to be kept to ourselves. It is meant to be shared because the world needs to know that hope exists beyond the pain, sin, and brokenness they experience.

In Matthew 28:19-20, Jesus gives the Great Commission, saying: "Go therefore and make disciples of all nations, baptizing them in the name of the Father and of the Son and of the Holy Spirit, teaching them to observe all things that I have commanded you." This command was not only for the disciples who walked with Jesus—it is for all believers throughout history. The responsibility to make disciples has been passed down through generations, and now it rests with you and me.

Sharing the Good News of redemption can feel daunting, especially in a world where people may seem indifferent or even resistant to the message. But we must remember that sharing the Gospel is not about having all the answers or persuading people to believe—it is about bearing witness to what God has done in our own lives. It is about telling others that we were lost but are now found, that we were dead in our sins but are now alive in Christ. Our lives serve as the most powerful testimony we have.

The call to share the Good News is not just about words—it is about actions as well. As believers, we are called to love, serve, and show Christ's compassion in tangible ways. Sometimes, the way we live speaks louder than the words we say. When we reflect Christ's love through our actions, it opens doors for conversations about the hope we have in Him. As 1 Peter 3:15 (NKJV) reminds us: "But sanctify the Lord God in your hearts, and always be ready to give a defense to everyone who asks you a reason for the hope that is in you, with meekness and fear."

This call to share the Good News extends beyond our local communities—it is a global mission. God's desire is for all people to be saved, and the redemption found in Jesus Christ is for everyone. Acts 1:8 declares: "But you shall receive power when the Holy Spirit has come upon you, and you shall be witnesses to Me in Jerusalem, and in all Judea and Samaria, and to the end of the earth." This means that our mission is not just to reach those closest to us, but to extend the message of redemption to every corner of the world.

The Good News of redemption is the most beautiful message we can share because it brings eternal hope. It is not just a message of temporary comfort—it is the promise of eternal life in God's presence. This message transforms hearts, heals brokenness, and restores relationships. When we share it, we participate in God's great work of redemption.

Whether through your words, actions, or prayers, you have a role in sharing the Good News of redemption. The world needs to hear it, and you are the messenger God has called to carry it. Every time you share the hope of Jesus with someone, you take part in the mission of bringing light into darkness, healing into brokenness, and life into death. This calling will not only shape your own life but also impact the lives of those around you, leading them to the redemption found only in Christ.

Reflection: How Has God's Redemptive Love Impacted Your Life? Take a moment to reflect on these:

How has understanding Christ's sacrifice transformed the way you approach God?

Do you find yourself striving to earn God's favor, or have you fully embraced the grace given through Christ's sacrifice?

In what areas of your life do you struggle to accept God's grace, and how can you surrender those areas to Him?

How does Christ's reconciliation with you inspire you to reconcile with others? Are there any relationships in your life that need healing?

As an ambassador for Christ, what steps can you take to share the message of reconciliation in your community?

What does it mean to you personally that Jesus bridged the gap between God and mankind? How does that change the way you live your daily life?

How do you live in the freedom Christ has given you? Are there areas where you still feel bound by sin? How can you walk in the victory Christ has provided?

What does it look like for you to live a life that reflects the reconciliation you've received from God?

How can you better prioritize your relationship with God in your daily routine?

What practical steps can you take to ensure that your life aligns with God's purpose and that you're living for His glory?

CHAPTER 5

Restored to Fellowship

"Behold, what manner of love the Father has bestowed on us, that we should be called children of God!" (1 John 3:1, NKJV)

THE RESTORATION OF FELLOWSHIP

The Bible teaches that God created humanity for fellowship—to live in a close, intimate relationship with Him. However, when sin entered the world, that perfect relationship was broken. Sin's consequences led to separation from God, leaving humanity in a desperate state. Yet, in His infinite mercy and love, God made a way for restoration.

In this chapter, we will explore what it means to be restored to fellowship with God through Jesus Christ. We'll examine the transformative power of God's love, the role of the Holy Spirit in empowering believers, and practical ways to deepen our relationship with Him.

LIVING AS CHILDREN OF GOD AND HEIRS TO HIS PROMISES

One of the most profound truths of the Christian faith is that through Jesus Christ, we are restored as children of God. We are no longer strangers or enemies of God but beloved sons and daughters. John 1:12 declares, "But as many as received Him, to them He gave the right to become children of God, to those who believe in His name" (NKJV).

When we accept Jesus Christ as our Lord and Savior, we are adopted into God's family. This adoption is more than just a change in status—it is a radical transformation of our identity. We move from being slaves to sin to becoming heirs of God's promises. As His children, we inherit the blessings that come with being part of His family.

Paul speaks about this inheritance in Romans 8:17: "And if children, then heirs—heirs of God and joint heirs with Christ, if indeed we suffer with Him, that we may also be glorified together" (NKJV). This inheritance is not merely something we await in the future; it is a reality we can begin to experience now as we walk in our identity as God's children.

Being a child of God also means we have direct access to Him as our Heavenly Father. Just as a child confidently approaches a loving parent, we, too, can come before God with boldness, knowing that He loves us and desires a close relationship with us. Jesus taught us to pray with the words, "Our Father in heaven" (Matthew 6:9, NKJV), a phrase that reflects the depth of intimacy God longs to share with us.

THE ROLE OF THE HOLY SPIRIT IN EMPOWERING BELIEVERS TO LIVE FOR GOD

One of the most precious gifts God has given us in restoring our fellowship with Him is the presence of the Holy Spirit. After Jesus ascended to heaven, He promised to send the Holy Spirit to be with His followers—to guide them and empower them for the work of His Kingdom.

In John 14:16-17, Jesus says, "And I will pray to the Father, and He will give you another Helper, that He may abide with you forever—the Spirit of truth, whom the world cannot receive because it neither sees Him nor knows Him; but you know Him, for He dwells with you and will be in you" (NKJV). The Holy Spirit is not only with us but also within us, equipping us to live according to God's will and fulfill our divine purpose.

The Role of the Holy Spirit in a Believer's Life

Conviction of Sin: The Holy Spirit convicts us of sin and guides us toward righteousness. His conviction is not meant to condemn but to lead us to repentance and healing.

Empowerment for Christian Living: The Holy Spirit strengthens us to live victoriously over sin. He enables us to walk in the fruit of the Spirit—producing love, joy, peace, patience, kindness, goodness, faithfulness, gentleness, and self-control (Galatians 5:22-23, NKJV).

Guidance: The Holy Spirit directs us in making decisions that honor God. He leads us daily, helping us discern His will. As Paul writes in Romans 8:14, "For as many as are led by the Spirit of God, these are sons of God" (NKJV).

Comfort and Encouragement: In times of trial, the Holy Spirit is our Comforter. He strengthens and encourages us, reminding us of God's promises and faithfulness.

Living in the power of the Holy Spirit is essential for walking in fellowship with God. Through the Spirit, we grow in our relationship with Him and live a life that reflects His glory.

STEPS TO DEEPEN YOUR RELATIONSHIP WITH GOD

Restored fellowship with God is not just a theological concept; it is a practical reality that influences every aspect of our lives. Like any relationship, fellowship with God requires intentional effort. Here are some practical steps to help strengthen your connection with Him:

Daily Prayer: Prayer is our primary means of communication with God. It's more than just presenting requests—it's about dwelling in His presence, listening to His voice, and sharing our hearts with Him. Set aside dedicated time each day for prayer to cultivate a deeper intimacy with God. "Draw near to God and He will draw near to you" (James 4:8, NKJV).

Bible Study: God speaks to us through His Word. Regular Bible study deepens our understanding of His character, will, and promises. As we immerse ourselves in Scripture, we grow closer to Him and gain wisdom for life's journey. "Your word is a lamp to my feet and a light to my path" (Psalm 119:105, NKJV).

Worship and Praise: Worship is an expression of love and gratitude to God. Whether through singing, dancing, or quiet meditation, worship draws us into deeper fellowship with Him. "Oh come, let us worship and bow down; let us kneel before the Lord our Maker" (Psalm 95:6, NKJV).

Obedience: True fellowship with God is reflected in our obedience to Him. Jesus said, "If you love Me, keep My commandments" (John 14:15, NKJV). Following God's Word is a tangible demonstration of our love and commitment to Him.

Fellowship with Other Believers: Engaging with other believers through church, Bible study groups, or fellowship gatherings is vital for spiritual growth. "As iron sharpens iron, so a man sharpens the countenance of his friend" (Proverbs 27:17, NKJV). Surrounding ourselves with fellow Christians encourages accountability, support, and mutual encouragement in our faith journey.

THE ROLE OF PRAYER IN RESTORED FELLOWSHIP

Prayer plays a vital role in restoring and deepening our fellowship with God. It is more than a ritual or a duty—it is a powerful and personal conversation with our Creator. When we view prayer through the lens of restored fellowship, it becomes a sacred means of reconnecting with God, sharing our hearts, and listening to His voice.

Before the fall, Adam and Eve walked with God in perfect communion. But sin fractured that relationship, making prayer essential for drawing near to Him again. Jesus' sacrifice on the cross bridged the gap, granting us direct access to God. Now, through prayer, we can approach Him boldly—just as children come to their loving Father. No longer bound by rituals or sacrifices, we can speak to God personally and freely because of what Jesus has done.

Prayer is not just about presenting our needs—it is about being present with God. It is a space where we can express our deepest concerns, joys, and burdens while also receiving His love, guidance, and peace. Through prayer, we confess our sins, receive His forgiveness, and realign our hearts with His will. It is an opportunity to pour out our hearts and then sit quietly, listening for His still, small voice.

Even in the most overwhelming moments of life, prayer reminds us that we are never alone. It is our lifeline to the One who created us and knows us intimately. Through prayer, our fellowship with God is not just restored—it is strengthened. In those sacred moments with Him, we experience His presence, receive His peace, and are transformed.

THE ASSURANCE OF GOD'S PRESENCE

The assurance of God's presence is one of the most profound and comforting aspects of our faith. In the busyness of life, in moments of joy, and in times of trial, knowing that God is with us brings a peace and security that nothing else can offer.

When we speak of the assurance of God's presence, we are not referring to a distant or abstract concept. It is a real, intimate connection with God in our everyday lives. He is not a far-off, detached figure but a loving Father who walks with us, guides us, and holds us close.

This assurance does not mean that life will be free of pain or challenges. Instead, it means that even in our darkest moments, God is with us, offering comfort, strength, and peace. In Isaiah 41:10, He promises, "Fear not, for I am with you; be not dismayed, for I am your God. I will strengthen you, yes, I will help you, I will uphold you with My righteous right hand." (NKJV). This is more than just a reassuring thought—it is a deep, personal promise from God.

At times, we may not immediately feel God's presence. There may be seasons when His voice seems silent, and we wonder where He is amid our struggles. But the truth is, God's presence is not dependent on our emotions. He is always with us, whether we sense it or not. Jesus reassures us in Matthew 28:20, "Lo, I am with you always, even to the end of the age." (NKJV). His presence is unwavering.

The assurance of God's presence means we are never truly alone. Whether we are walking through a season of joy or facing hardship, His presence provides the peace and strength we need. We can rest in the truth that He is with us—guiding our steps, comforting our hearts, and reminding us that His love never fades.

THE RESTORATION OF JOY IN FELLOWSHIP

When sin entered the world, it not only disrupted our relationship with God but also robbed us of the deep, unshakable joy that comes from being in close communion with Him. Yet through Christ, that joy is restored.

Imagine walking in perfect harmony with God, as Adam and Eve did in the Garden of Eden before the fall—no distance, no shame, no brokenness. They experienced true joy because they were fully in His presence, living out their purpose as His beloved creation. Their joy was not a fleeting emotion but a deep, soul-satisfying peace that came from perfect fellowship with their Creator.

When Jesus came, He bridged the gap between humanity and God, restoring the relationship that had been fractured by sin. In John 15:11, Jesus says, "These things I have spoken to you, that My joy may remain in you, and that your joy may be full." (NKJV). Through Christ's sacrifice and the work of the Holy Spirit, we are invited back into that intimate relationship with God—where joy is not an abstract concept but a real, tangible experience.

The restoration of joy in fellowship is not about mere happiness or fleeting emotions. It is a deep, abiding peace that comes from knowing we are loved by God and welcomed into His presence. When we spend time with Him—whether through prayer, worship, or quiet moments in His presence—His joy fills our hearts. It is a joy that surpasses understanding, one that does not depend on circumstances but flows from the unshakable truth that we are His, and He is ours.

In the Psalms, David often speaks of the joy found in God's presence. In Psalm 16:11, he declares, "You will show me the path of life; in Your presence is fullness of joy; at Your right hand are pleasures forevermore." (NKJV). This is the joy that comes from fellowship with God—a joy that is full, complete, and eternal.

As we grow in our relationship with God, the joy of fellowship becomes more evident in our daily lives. This does not mean life will be free of challenges, but it does mean that even amid trials, there is a joy that remains. It is the joy of knowing that God is with us, guiding us, and loving us unconditionally. And once restored, that joy becomes a testimony of His goodness to the world around us.

THE INVITATION TO INTIMACY

The invitation to intimacy with God is one of the most profound expressions of His love for us. From the very beginning, God has desired to draw us close—not as distant subjects, but as beloved children and friends. This invitation isn't about a superficial relationship; it is a deep, personal, and transformative connection that shapes every part of our lives.

God's invitation to intimacy is woven throughout Scripture. In Revelation 3:20, Jesus says, "Behold, I stand at the door and knock. If anyone hears My voice and opens the door, I will come in to him and dine with him, and he with Me." (NKJV). The imagery of dining together reflects the kind of relationship God desires—a close, personal communion where we share our hearts with Him and receive His love and guidance.

This invitation is not limited by our imperfections or past mistakes. God draws near to us despite our flaws. His love is unconditional, and His arms are always open. The story of the prodigal son in Luke 15 is a perfect example. The father does not wait for his son to reach the door; he runs to him, embraces him, and restores him. This is God's heart toward us—He longs to be close to us, no matter where we have been or what we have done.

Living in intimacy with God means more than just knowing about Him—it means knowing Him personally. It involves spending time in His presence, listening to His voice, and allowing His Spirit to guide us. It is about trusting Him with our joys and fears, our hopes and struggles, and letting Him speak life into every area of our hearts.

This relationship is not one-sided. As we draw near to God, He draws near to us. James 4:8 reminds us, "Draw near to God and He will draw near to you." (NKJV). This is His promise. He meets us where we are, and in His presence, we find peace, joy, and the fulfillment our souls long for.

Intimacy with God transforms us. It deepens our understanding of His love and shapes our identity. It empowers us to live confidently, knowing we are deeply loved and fully known. This intimacy is not a distant hope—it is an invitation available to us every single day. All we have to do is respond, opening our hearts and lives to the One who loves us most.

FELLOWSHIP AS THE SOURCE OF STRENGTH AND ENCOURAGEMENT

Fellowship with God is the wellspring of strength and encouragement for the believer. In His presence, we find reassurance, guidance, and the power to navigate life's challenges. This connection is not just a spiritual concept—it is a tangible source of renewal that equips us to face each day with confidence and hope.

When we spend time in fellowship with God, we are reminded of His promises. Scripture is filled with affirmations of His faithfulness and care, and in His presence, those truths come alive in our hearts. Isaiah 41:10 reassures us: "Fear not, for I am with you; be not dismayed, for I am your God. I will strengthen you, yes, I will help you, I will uphold you with My righteous right hand." (NKJV). Knowing that God is with us provides a profound sense of security and empowerment, especially in moments of weakness or doubt.

Fellowship with God also renews our perspective. In the busyness of life, it is easy to become overwhelmed or lose sight of the bigger picture. However, when we draw near to Him, He realigns our focus, reminding us of His sovereignty and the hope we have in Him. Psalm 16:11 declares, "You will show me the path of life; in Your presence is fullness of joy; at Your right hand are pleasures forevermore." (NKJV). In His presence, we find not only strength but also the encouragement to press on with joy.

Moreover, fellowship with God is where we receive His peace—a peace that transcends circumstances. Philippians 4:6–7 urges us to bring our anxieties to God in prayer. As we do, His peace guards our hearts and minds, strengthening us to face uncertainty and adversity with courage, knowing that He is in control.

This fellowship not only strengthens us individually but also inspires us to encourage others. As we experience God's love and grace, we are empowered to extend the same to those around us. Our time with Him fills us so that we can pour into others, becoming conduits of His strength and encouragement.

Ultimately, fellowship with God is not a one-time event but a continual process. Daily moments in prayer, worship, and reflection keep us connected to the true source of our strength. It is in His presence that we find the encouragement to persevere, the wisdom to navigate challenges, and the assurance that we are never alone. This fellowship sustains us, uplifts us, and propels us forward in faith.

Reflection: What Steps Can You Take to Strengthen Your Fellowship with God?

Reflect on These Questions:

How does the promise of eternal fellowship with God shape the way you live today?

In what ways can you cultivate a deeper awareness of God's presence in your daily routine?

What barriers in your life might hinder your fellowship with God, and how can you overcome them?

How does the assurance of God's eternal presence bring you hope in times of struggle or uncertainty?

What does it mean to you personally that God desires an intimate and eternal relationship with you?

How can you encourage others to seek and cherish fellowship with God in their own lives?

How does the vision of ultimate fellowship with God shape your perspective on temporary challenges and trials?

Do you need to set aside more time for prayer and Bible study?

Is there an area of your life where God is calling you to deeper obedience?

Are there fellow believers who can help you grow in your faith?

CHAPTER 6

Living Out God's Purpose

"For we are His workmanship, created in Christ Jesus for good works, which God prepared beforehand that we should walk in them." (Ephesians 2:10, NKJV)

EMBRACING YOUR DIVINE CALLING

Then God created us, He did so with intentionality and purpose. We are not accidents or random beings; we are His masterpiece, uniquely designed to fulfill His divine plan. Every believer is called to walk in the good works that God has prepared in advance. Understanding and embracing God's purpose for our lives is the key to fulfilling our divine calling.

This chapter will guide you in discovering your purpose, living as a reflection of God's glory, and trusting in His ultimate plan for both your life and eternity.

DISCOVERING AND WALKING IN YOUR GOD-GIVEN PURPOSE

One of the most profound questions we can ask ourselves is: "What is my purpose?" It's natural to wonder about the meaning of our lives and the unique gifts and talents God has given us. Fortunately, the Bible assures us that we are created with a specific purpose in mind.

Ephesians 2:10 reminds us, "For we are His workmanship, created in Christ Jesus for good works, which God prepared beforehand that we should walk in them." (NKJV)

This verse reveals two important truths:

We are God's workmanship – God, the ultimate Creator, has designed us with care, precision, and love. Our lives are a reflection of His creative genius. Each of us is a masterpiece, intentionally crafted for a specific purpose.

We are created for good works – The good works God has prepared for us are not random tasks; they are the very reason for which we were created. He has a plan for each of us—assignments that align with His greater Kingdom purpose.

Discovering your God-given purpose begins with listening to the Holy Spirit. He guides us, reveals God's plans, and helps us discern our unique calling. Through prayer, meditation on God's Word, and seeking wise counsel from other believers, we gain clarity about His direction for our lives. Often, God's purpose is revealed through the passions, gifts, and talents He has placed within us.

For example, if you have a heart for teaching, God may be calling you to instruct others in His Word, mentor, or disciple. If you have a passion for healing, perhaps He is leading you to become a caregiver, doctor, or counsellor. God's calling is as unique as you are, and it often involves using your natural gifts to serve Him and others.

LIVING AS A LIGHT IN THE WORLD AND REFLECTING GOD'S GLORY

As we walk in our God-given purpose, we are called to be a light in the world. In Matthew 5:14, Jesus says, "You are the light of the world. A city that is set on a hill cannot be hidden." (NKJV) Our lives should radiate God's love, truth, and grace, drawing others to Him. The purpose of our good works is not to bring attention to ourselves but to reflect God's glory.

Living as a light in the world means actively seeking to influence those around us for Christ. We do this by embodying the values of the Kingdom—love, kindness, truth, justice, and humility. As we live according to these principles, we become living testimonies of God's transformative power.

One way to shine as a light is by being intentional in our relationships. Whether in our families, workplaces, or communities, we are called to be salt and light. Our actions, words, and attitudes should reflect God's love and truth, demonstrating what it means to follow Christ. Paul writes in Philippians 2:15, "That you may become blameless and harmless, children of God without fault in the midst of a crooked and perverse generation, among whom you shine as lights in the world." (NKJV)

Living as a light also means serving others. 1 Peter 4:10 reminds us, "As each one has received a gift, minister it to one another, as good stewards of the manifold grace of God." (NKJV) When we use our gifts to serve, we reflect the heart of God, demonstrating selfless love to the world.

TRUSTING IN GOD'S ULTIMATE PLAN FOR YOUR LIFE AND ETERNITY

Living out God's purpose is not always easy. There will be challenges, setbacks, and moments of doubt. However, as we walk in faith, we must trust that God's plan for our lives is perfect—both for our time on earth and for eternity.

Romans 8:28 assures us, "And we know that all things work together for good to those who love God, to those who are the called according to His purpose." (NKJV) Even when life doesn't unfold as we expect, we can trust that God is working behind the scenes to bring about His divine purposes. His plan is not limited to this life; it extends into eternity.

The ultimate fulfillment of God's purpose for us is not about earthly success or achievements—it is about eternal life with Him. As we pursue our calling on earth, we are preparing for the glory that awaits us in Heaven. Paul reminds us in 2 Corinthians 4:17, "For our light affliction, which is but for a moment, is working for us a far more exceeding and eternal weight of glory." (NKJV)

God's purpose for our lives is greater than we can fully comprehend. Trusting in His plan requires faith, surrender, and obedience. Even when we don't understand why certain things happen, we can rest in the truth that He is working all things together for His glory and our ultimate good.

1. Embracing Your Uniqueness In God's Purpose
You Are Chosen by Design

God's purpose for you is both specific and intentional. Ephesians 1:4 affirms that we were chosen in Christ before the foundation of the world to be holy and blameless. Your individuality is not an accident—it is an essential part of His perfect design.

Example: Consider biblical figures like Moses, Esther, and David—each had unique backgrounds, abilities, and circumstances that played a vital role in fulfilling God's plan for their lives. Likewise, your gifts and experiences are intentionally crafted to serve His divine purpose.

Avoid Comparison

Comparison is one of the greatest obstacles to embracing God's purpose for your life. When you measure yourself against others, it can lead to discouragement or pride, pulling your focus away from God's unique calling for you. Instead of looking at what others are doing, center your attention on your personal journey with Him.

Galatians 6:4 reminds us, "But let each one examine his own work, and then he will have rejoicing in himself alone, and not in another." (NKJV) Your walk with God is unique—trust that He has equipped you with everything you need for the path He has set before you.

2. Fulfilling Your Role As God's Workmanship

Good Works Are Part of Your Calling

Ephesians 2:10 reminds us that we are created in Christ Jesus for good works. These works are not a means of earning salvation but a response to the grace we have received. As believers, we are called to reflect God's love through our actions, demonstrating our faith in practical ways.

Practical Examples of Good Works

Volunteering in your church or community to serve others with love and humility.

Mentoring or discipling individuals who are growing in their faith.

Sharing your testimony to encourage and guide those who do not yet know Christ.

Impacting Future Generations

Living out your purpose has a ripple effect. Your faith, actions, and legacy can inspire others to seek and follow God's plan for their lives. The choices you make today can influence future generations, fostering a heritage of faith and obedience to God's calling.

3. Obstacles To Living Out God's Purpose

Fear and Doubt

Many people hesitate to walk in their purpose because of fear or feelings of inadequacy. However, God reassures us in Isaiah 41:10:

"Fear not, for I am with you; be not dismayed, for I am your God. I will strengthen you, yes, I will help you."

Overcoming Fear:

Pray for boldness and take small, obedient steps of faith.

Trust that God's presence and strength will sustain you.

Distractions of the World

The busyness and temptations of life can pull you away from God's purpose. It is crucial to prioritize your relationship with Him and seek His kingdom first. As Matthew 6:33 instructs: "But seek first the kingdom of God and His righteousness, and all these things shall be added to you."

Overcoming Distractions:

Set aside dedicated time for prayer and studying God's Word.

Create intentional habits that keep your focus on Him.

Lack of Faith

Fulfilling your purpose often requires stepping into the unknown. Trust that God equips those He calls and will guide you every step of the way. When faced with uncertainty, remember Hebrews 11:1: "Now faith is the substance of things hoped for, the evidence of things not seen."

Strengthening Your Faith:

Surround yourself with a community of believers who encourage and uplift you.

Reflect on God's past faithfulness as a reminder of His trustworthiness.

A LIFE THAT REFLECTS GOD'S GLORY

Shining Brightly in a Dark World

Jesus calls us to be the salt of the earth and the light of the world (Matthew 5:13–16). This involves living a life that glorifies God and attracts others to Him.

Your character, integrity, and love for others are powerful testimonies of God's work in your life.

Living with Eternal Perspective

Recognize that your purpose goes beyond this life. Every act of obedience and faithfulness contributes to God's eternal kingdom.

The Ultimate Goal

The chief purpose of humanity is to glorify God and enjoy Him forever. Living out your purpose allows you to experience the fullness of His joy and peace.

Walking Daily in God's Purpose

Daily Surrender

Living out God's purpose begins with daily surrender. Jesus taught us to pray, "Your will be done" (Matthew 6:10). This requires letting go of our plans and trusting God's direction.

Step to take:

Begin each day with prayer, asking God to guide your actions, thoughts, and decisions.

Small Acts of Faithfulness

Fulfilling your purpose doesn't always involve grand gestures. Often, it's the small, faithful acts that make a significant impact.

Examples include showing kindness to a neighbor, speaking words of encouragement, or offering to pray for someone in need.

Luke 16:10 reminds us, "He who is faithful in what is least is faithful also in much."

4. Recognizing Divine Opportunities

Be Open to Interruptions

God often works through unexpected moments. Be sensitive to the Holy Spirit's prompting, even when it feels inconvenient.

Example: The Good Samaritan (Luke 10:25–37) was willing to pause his journey to help someone in need.

Viewing Your Workplace or Community as a Mission Field

Your purpose isn't confined to the church. God places you in specific environments to be a light.

Colossians 3:23 encourages us to work wholeheartedly as if serving the Lord.

Share Christ's love through your work ethic, integrity, and interactions with others.

5. Discovering Your Spiritual Gifts

Identifying Your Gifts

Every believer has been given spiritual gifts to serve the body of Christ and advance God's kingdom.

Romans 12:6–8 and 1 Corinthians 12 provide insight into these gifts, which may include teaching, encouragement, hospitality, or leadership.

Using Your Gifts for God's Glory

Your gifts are not meant for personal gain but for building up others.

Practical Step: Volunteer in your church or community to discover how your gifts can meet the needs of others.

6. Facing Challenges with Purpose

Trials as Opportunities for Growth

Challenges can strengthen your faith and refine your character. James 1:2–4 encourages us to "consider it pure joy" when we face trials, as they develop perseverance and spiritual maturity.

Instead of asking "Why is this happening?" shift your perspective and seek what God wants to teach you in difficult seasons.

Overcoming Resistance and Opposition

Pursuing your God-given purpose may invite criticism, setbacks, or even spiritual opposition. However, 2 Corinthians 12:9 reminds us that God's strength is made perfect in our weakness.

Encouragement: Stay rooted in God's Word and surround yourself with a faith-filled community that uplifts and supports you in times of struggle.

Reflecting God's Glory in Relationships

Love as the Foundation

Jesus said the greatest commandments are to love God and love others (Matthew 22:37–39). Fulfilling your purpose means cultivating relationships that reflect His love.

Prioritize **forgiveness, patience, and understanding** in your interactions, even when it's difficult. Love is the foundation of Christ-centered relationships.

2. Mentoring and Discipleship

As you walk in your purpose, invest in others by mentoring and discipling them. Paul's relationship with Timothy serves as a model for guiding others in faith (2 Timothy 2:2).

Practical Step: Look for opportunities to pour wisdom and encouragement into others, helping them grow in their walk with Christ.

7. Celebrating God's Plan for Your Life

Gratitude for God's Faithfulness

Take time to reflect on how far God has brought you and express gratitude for His guidance. A heart of thankfulness strengthens your faith and keeps your focus on His goodness.

Psalm 107:1 declares, "Oh, give thanks to the Lord, for He is good! For His mercy endures forever."

Anticipating Future Fulfillment

God's purpose for your life is not confined to the present—it extends into eternity. The ultimate fulfillment of His plan is spending forever in His presence.

Revelation 21:3–4 reminds us of the joy that awaits when God dwells with His people, wiping away every tear and removing sorrow forever.

Walking in God's Purpose Through Seasons of Life

God's Purpose in Every Season

Life unfolds in different seasons—times of growth, waiting, pruning, and harvest. Recognizing that God's purpose is present in every stage helps you stay faithful, even when you don't see the full picture.

Ecclesiastes 3:1 affirms, "To everything there is a season, a time for every purpose under heaven."

Encouragement: In seasons of waiting, trust God's timing. In seasons of action,

8. **step forward with boldness.**

Biblical Examples of God's Purpose in Seasons

Moses: Spent 40 years in the wilderness before leading Israel out of Egypt, demonstrating that seasons of preparation are essential for fulfilling God's plan.

Esther: Positioned as queen "for such a time as this" (Esther 4:14), showing that God places us in specific roles for His divine purpose.

Joseph: Endured betrayal, slavery, and imprisonment before stepping into leadership in Egypt, proving that hardships can be stepping stones to greater fulfillment.

9. Balancing Your Purpose with Everyday Responsibilities

Living with Intentionality

God's purpose is not separate from your daily life but woven into it. Your work, responsibilities, and service are opportunities to glorify Him.

1 Corinthians 10:31 reminds us, "Whether you eat or drink, or whatever you do, do all to the glory of God."

Balancing Spiritual Growth and Practical Tasks

Prioritize time with God through prayer, worship, and studying His Word to maintain spiritual growth.

Integrate faith into everyday activities—pray while cooking, meditate on Scripture during your commute, or worship as you complete daily tasks.

10. Fulfilling Your Purpose in the Body of Christ

Unity in Diversity

Each believer has a unique role within the body of Christ. Together, these roles work in harmony to fulfil God's will.

1 Corinthians 12:12 teaches, "For as the body is one and has many members, but all the members of that one body, being many, are one body, so is Christ."

Serving the Church and Community

Find ways to serve within your church through teaching, outreach, or administrative support.

Extend service beyond the church by engaging in community efforts, mentoring youth, or volunteering for causes that align with God's values.

11. Overcoming Barriers to Fulfilling God's Purpose

Self-Doubt and Insecurity

Many struggle to believe they are capable of fulfilling God's purpose. Even Moses doubted his ability to lead, but God reassured him, "I will certainly be with you" (Exodus 3:12).

Encouragement: Rely on God's strength rather than your own abilities.

Fear of Failure

Fear often paralyzes people from stepping out in faith. However, 2 Timothy 1:7 reminds us, "For God has not given us a spirit of fear, but of power and love and a sound mind."

Action Step: Replace fear with trust in God's sovereignty and grace.

Distractions and Busyness

Modern life is filled with distractions that can pull you away from God's purpose. Jesus reminds us to "seek first the kingdom of God" (Matthew 6:33).

Practical Step: Regularly evaluate your priorities and remove commitments that hinder your spiritual growth.

12. Leaving a Legacy of Purpose

Impacting Future Generations

Walking in God's purpose allows you to leave a lasting legacy of faith. Abraham's obedience led to blessings for countless generations.

Deuteronomy 7:9: "Know that the Lord your God, He is God, the faithful God who keeps covenant and mercy for a thousand generations with those who love Him and keep His commandments."

Mentoring and Discipling Others

Pass on wisdom and experiences by mentoring others in their walk with Christ.

Paul's relationship with Timothy exemplifies this:

2 Timothy 2:2: "And the things that you have heard from me among many witnesses, commit these to faithful men who will be able to teach others also."

13. Reflection and Application

Journaling Your Journey

Encourage readers to reflect on their spiritual journey by journaling how they have experienced God's purpose.

What moments in your life revealed God's purpose most clearly?

How can you align your daily decisions with God's plan?

Creating a Personal Purpose Statement

Invite readers to write a personal purpose statement based on prayer, scripture, and reflection.

Example: "I exist to glorify God by [specific actions or calling], empowered by His love and grace."

14. **Biblical Examples of Purpose**

Joseph: From Pit to Palace

Joseph's story illustrates how God can use difficulties to fulfill a greater purpose. Despite betrayal, slavery, and imprisonment, Joseph remained faithful, and God elevated him to a position where he could save many lives.

Genesis 50:20: "But as for you, you meant evil against me; but God meant it for good, to bring it about as it is this day, to save many people alive."

Lesson: God's purpose often requires patience and trust in His timing, even when the process seems painful or unfair.

Esther: Positioned for a Purpose

Esther's story reveals how God strategically places individuals to fulfill His will. As queen, she had to summon great courage to approach the king and intercede for her people.

Esther 4:14: "For if you remain completely silent at this time, relief and deliverance will arise for the Jews from another place, but you and your father's house will perish. Yet who knows whether you have come to the kingdom for such a time as this?"

Lesson: God equips us with courage and resources to fulfill His purpose, especially when the stakes are high.

Moses: Called to Lead

Despite his initial reluctance and self-doubt, Moses was chosen by God to lead the Israelites out of Egypt.

Exodus 3:10: "Come now, therefore, and I will send you to Pharaoh that you may bring My people, the children of Israel, out of Egypt."

Lesson: God's purpose often requires stepping out of one's comfort zone and relying on His power rather than one's abilities.

15 Paul: From Persecutor to Preacher

Paul's transformation from a persecutor of Christians to a key figure in spreading the gospel demonstrates God's power to redeem and repurpose lives.

Acts 9:15: "But the Lord said to him, 'Go, for he is a chosen vessel of Mine to bear My name before Gentiles, kings, and the children of Israel.'"

Lesson: No one is beyond God's ability to use. Your past mistakes do not disqualify you from fulfilling His calling.

David: A Shepherd Turned King

David's journey from tending sheep to becoming Israel's king demonstrates how God prepares individuals in humble, unseen ways before elevating them to positions of influence.

1 Samuel 13:14: "The Lord has sought for Himself a man after His own heart, and the Lord has commanded him to be commander over His people."

Lesson: Faithfulness in small responsibilities prepares us for greater purposes. If you are faithful in little, bigger responsibilities will be entrusted to you.

Jesus: The Ultimate Example of Purpose

Jesus' life and ministry were entirely focused on fulfilling God's purpose: to redeem humanity and restore fellowship with the Father.

Luke 19:10: "For the Son of Man has come to seek and to save that which was lost."

Lesson: Jesus is our perfect example. Living out God's purpose is a journey, not a destination. Even when the path seems unclear, God's presence is constant.

"For the Son of Man has come to seek and to save that which was lost." (Luke 19:10, NKJV)

Jesus exemplifies the ultimate surrender to God's will, even when it requires sacrifice. He calls believers to follow His example through obedience and love. As our perfect model, Jesus shows us that living out God's purpose is a journey, not a destination. Even when the path seems uncertain, God's presence remains constant. Trust Him to guide your steps as you embrace your calling to reflect His love and glory in the world.

"Commit your works to the Lord, and your thoughts will be established." (Proverbs 16:3, NKJV)

Misconceptions About Purpose

In the journey of discovering and living out God's purpose, several misconceptions can cloud our understanding and hinder fulfillment. These misunderstandings may lead to confusion, frustration, or doubt. However, by addressing them, we can better align our hearts and minds with God's true calling. Let's explore some of the most common misconceptions:

Purpose Is Only About Ministry or Church Work

Many believe that fulfilling God's purpose means serving in full-time ministry or holding a leadership role in the church. While ministry is one way to live out God's calling, His purpose is not confined to church-related roles.

Truth: God's purpose extends to all areas of life, including careers, relationships, and personal growth. Whether you are a teacher, entrepreneur, healthcare worker, or stay-at-home parent, God can use you to reflect His glory and fulfill His will.

"For we are His workmanship, created in Christ Jesus for good works, which God prepared beforehand that we should walk in them." (Ephesians 2:10, NKJV)

Purpose Is Only About Big, Grand Achievements

Some believe that purpose must involve something monumental, like writing a bestselling book, leading a global organization, or becoming a well-known speaker. This mindset can lead to frustration, especially when life feels ordinary or achievements seem small.

Truth: God often works through the small, everyday moments. Purpose is more about faithfulness and obedience than worldly success or recognition. Even the smallest acts of kindness and service matter in His kingdom.

"Do not despise these small beginnings, for the Lord rejoices to see the work begin." (Zechariah 4:10, NLT)

Purpose Is Fixed and Unchanging

Some believe that once they discover their purpose, it remains the same for life. This misconception can cause fear or stagnation, especially when circumstances change, and previous roles or callings no longer feel relevant.

Truth: God's purpose unfolds over time. As we grow in faith, He may lead us in new directions or call us to different areas of service. Being flexible and open to His leading is essential.

"A man's heart plans his way, but the Lord directs his steps." (Proverbs 16:9, NKJV)

Purpose Is All About Personal Fulfillment

Many associate purpose with personal happiness and fulfillment. While pursuing God's purpose brings joy, it is not centered on self-gratification but on glorifying God and serving others.

Truth: True fulfillment comes when we align our desires with God's will. Purpose often requires sacrifice and challenges that foster spiritual growth.

"Then Jesus said to His disciples, 'If anyone desires to come after Me, let him deny himself, and take up his cross, and follow Me.'" (Matthew 16:24, NKJV)

Purpose Is Only for the "Qualified" or "Special" People

A common misconception is that only pastors, missionaries, or those with theological training are called to fulfill a divine purpose. This belief can make others feel inadequate or unworthy.

Truth:

God calls all believers, regardless of background, to fulfill His purpose. He equips each person with unique gifts, talents, and passions to be used for His glory.

"But you are a chosen generation, a royal priesthood, a holy nation, His special people, that you may proclaim the praises of Him who called you out of darkness into His marvelous light." (1 Peter 2:9, NKJV)

Purpose Is Always Clear and Easy to Understand

Some expect their purpose to be revealed instantly and clearly. They anticipate a dramatic moment where everything suddenly makes sense.

Truth: For some, purpose is clear from the start, but for others, it is discovered gradually through prayer, reflection, and life experiences. Trusting God in the process is essential.

"For we walk by faith, not by sight." (2 Corinthians 5:7, NKJV)

Purpose Requires Perfection

Some believe they must be perfect before they can fulfill God's purpose. This can lead to feelings of unworthiness or a fear of failure.

Truth: God does not require perfection. He calls us as we are and uses our weaknesses to reveal His strength and grace.

"But He said to me, 'My grace is sufficient for you, for My strength is made perfect in weakness.' Therefore most gladly I will rather boast in my infirmities, that the power of Christ may rest upon me." (2 Corinthians 12:9, NKJV)

As you continue your journey to discover and live out God's purpose, consider whether any of these misconceptions have shaped your understanding. God's calling is diverse, dynamic, and far greater than we can imagine. Surrender your expectations, trust in His guidance, and allow Him to lead you into the unique purpose He has designed for your life.

Practical Tools for Discovering Purpose

Discovering and walking in God's purpose for your life can feel overwhelming, but it is a journey that can be navigated with intention and clarity. By using practical tools, you can uncover your purpose, stay aligned with God's plan, and walk in the fullness of what He has designed for you.

Prayer and Meditation on God's Word

Consistent Prayer and Reflection

Prayer is the most direct way to communicate with God and invite Him into the process of discovering your purpose. Through prayer, you align your heart with His will and seek His guidance. Meditation on Scripture helps center your thoughts on His promises, deepening your understanding of His character and calling for your life.

Steps to Take:

Set aside a specific time each day for quiet prayer and reflection.

Ask God specific questions about your purpose and role in His kingdom.

Meditate on key scriptures (e.g., Jeremiah 29:11, Ephesians 2:10, Romans 8:28) that speak to God's will for your life.

Write down any thoughts, feelings, or scriptures that come to you during prayer time.

"If any of you lacks wisdom, let him ask of God, who gives to all liberally and without reproach, and it will be given to him." (James 1:5, NKJV)

Discover Your Spiritual Gifts

God has equipped every believer with spiritual gifts that align with their purpose. These gifts serve as tools for ministry and service, helping you fulfill His calling in your life. By identifying your spiritual gifts, you can gain deeper insight into how and where God is leading you to serve and make an impact.

Steps to Take:

Take a spiritual gifts test (many are available online or through church resources).

Reflect on areas where you feel energized or passionate—whether in teaching, serving, encouraging, leadership, or other roles.

Seek guidance from trusted mentors or church leaders to better understand how you can apply your gifts in ministry or daily life.

"As each one has received a gift, minister it to one another, as good stewards of the manifold grace of God." (1 Peter 4:10, NKJV)

ASSESS YOUR PASSIONS AND INTERESTS

Passion and Interest Inventory

Your passions and interests often reflect the unique calling God has placed on your life. Paying attention to the things that stir your heart, excite you, or challenge you can help you identify areas where God is leading you to serve.

Steps to Take:

List your interests and passions—what activities make you feel most alive and purposeful?

Reflect on past experiences where you felt deeply fulfilled and in alignment with your calling.

Pray over your passions, asking God to confirm whether they align with His purpose for your life.

"Delight yourself also in the Lord, and He shall give you the desires of your heart." (Psalm 37:4, NKJV)

SEEK WISE COUNSEL

Mentorship and Accountability

Mentors and trusted individuals can offer invaluable insight as you navigate your journey of discovering God's purpose. Their wisdom, experience, and guidance can help you gain a fresh perspective, provide encouragement, and offer correction when needed.

Steps to Take:

Seek a mentor or spiritual advisor who has experience walking in God's purpose and can offer biblical guidance.

Regularly meet with a trusted group or individual for accountability, prayer, and support.

Remain open to feedback and constructive challenge from those who know you well and can speak truth into your life.

"Without counsel, plans go awry, but in the multitude of counselors they are established." (Proverbs 15:22, NKJV)

ALIGN YOUR LIFE WITH GOD'S WORD

Biblical Alignment and Action Plan

God's Word serves as the ultimate blueprint for your life. Aligning your actions, thoughts, and desires with Scripture ensures that you are walking in His purpose. Regularly studying the Bible and applying its principles will help you stay connected to God's vision for you.

Steps to Take:

Commit to daily Bible reading and reflection, focusing on scriptures that reveal God's will and purpose.

Develop an action plan rooted in biblical principles that align with your gifts, passions, and calling.

Regularly evaluate how well your life reflects God's truth and purpose, making necessary adjustments to stay aligned with His Word.

"Your word is a lamp to my feet and a light to my path." (Psalm 119:105, NKJV)

EMBRACE LIFE'S CHALLENGES AND EXPERIENCES

Reflection on Life Experiences

Both positive and challenging life experiences are often part of God's shaping process in revealing your purpose. Reflecting on these moments and recognizing how God has used them can provide valuable insight into the direction He wants you to go.

Steps to Take:

Reflect on key moments in your life that have shaped your character, skills, or understanding of the world.

Ask God to help you see how these experiences can be used for His kingdom.

Look for recurring patterns in your life that may indicate a specific calling or purpose.

"And we know that all things work together for good to those who love God, to those who are the called according to His purpose." (Romans 8:28, NKJV)

STEP OUT IN FAITH

Faith-Based Action

Discovering and fulfilling your purpose often requires taking bold steps of faith, even when the path ahead isn't entirely clear. Trusting God and stepping out in obedience—despite uncertainty—allows Him to guide you and reveal more of your purpose as you move forward.

Steps to Take:

Identify one area where you feel God is calling you to take a step of faith.

Trust God with the next step, even if you don't fully understand where He's leading.

Take action, knowing that as you seek His will, He will direct your steps.

"Trust in the Lord with all your heart, and lean not on your own understanding; in all your ways acknowledge Him, and He shall direct your paths." (Proverbs 3:5-6, NKJV)

As you apply these practical tools in your life, remain patient and trust in God's perfect timing. Discovering your purpose is a journey that unfolds over time, and each step of faith brings you closer to the fullness of the life God has designed for you. Stay open, keep seeking, and remember—God is with you every step of the way.

DEALING WITH CHALLENGES IN LIVING OUT PURPOSE

Overcoming Challenges in Fulfilling God's Purpose

Living out your God-given purpose is a fulfilling and rewarding journey, but it's not without its challenges. Every believer encounters obstacles along the way—whether in the form of doubt, fear, distractions, or even opposition from others. How you respond to these challenges determines how effectively you walk in your purpose.

Here's how to navigate some common challenges in fulfilling God's calling for your life:

DOUBT AND UNCERTAINTY

1. Challenge:

Doubt about whether you're on the right path or truly walking in God's purpose can be one of the most paralyzing obstacles. At times, you may question if you have heard God correctly or wonder whether you're equipped for the task He has set before you.

HOW TO OVERCOME:

Trust God's Guidance: Believe that God will lead you and that He has equipped you for what He's called you to do. His Word assures us that He will never leave nor forsake us (Hebrews 13:5).

Revisit God's Promises: Reflect on scriptures that affirm His plans for your life (Jeremiah 29:11, Isaiah 55:11). When doubt arises, remind yourself that God's purposes are steadfast and that He is faithful to bring them to completion.

Act in Faith: Sometimes, the best way to overcome doubt is to take a step of faith. Trust that as you walk in obedience, God will direct your steps.

"Trust in the Lord with all your heart, and lean not on your own understanding; in all your ways acknowledge Him, and He shall direct your paths." (Proverbs 3:5-6, NKJV)

FEAR OF FAILURE

1. **Challenge:**

The fear of failure or not measuring up can prevent you from wholeheartedly pursuing your purpose. Worrying about making mistakes, disappointing others, or not succeeding can keep you from stepping into your calling.

How to Overcome:

Embrace God's Grace: Recognize that God's grace covers you, and He is not expecting perfection. He values obedience and trust more than flawless execution (Philippians 1:6).

Shift Your Perspective: Instead of fearing failure, see it as an opportunity to learn and grow. Remember that failure is often a stepping stone to spiritual and personal development, and God can use all things for your good.

Start Small: Take small steps that align with God's purpose. As you see Him working in your life, your confidence will grow, and your fear will diminish.

"I can do all things through Christ who strengthens me." (Philippians 4:13, NKJV)

DISTRACTIONS AND BUSYNESS

1. **Challenge:**

Life is full of distractions—relationships, social media, and daily responsibilities—that can pull you away from focusing on God's purpose. A busy schedule can cause you to lose sight of your calling or feel overwhelmed by everything that demands your attention.

How to Overcome:

Prioritize Time with God: Commit to regular prayer, Bible study, and reflection. Setting aside time for spiritual disciplines helps you stay focused on God's purpose.

Simplify Your Life: Identify and eliminate distractions that hinder your spiritual growth. Consider streamlining your commitments to make room for what truly matters.

Set Boundaries: Be intentional with your time. Learn to say "no" to things that aren't aligned with your purpose so you can focus on what God has called you to do.

"But seek first the kingdom of God and His righteousness, and all these things shall be added to you." (Matthew 6:33, NKJV)

Overcoming Challenges in Fulfilling God's Purpose

Fulfilling your God-given purpose is a journey filled with rewards, but it also comes with challenges. Whether you face opposition, lack resources, or experience spiritual fatigue, how you respond to these obstacles will shape your ability to walk in your calling.

Here's how to navigate some common challenges along the way:

OPPOSITION FROM OTHERS

Challenge:

When you step into your purpose, not everyone will understand or support your calling. Opposition can come in the form of criticism, jealousy, or discouragement from others.

How to Overcome:

Stand Firm in Your Calling: Trust that God has called you, and remember that His opinion is what matters most. Be confident in your identity in Christ and in the work He has set before you.

Respond with Grace: When faced with opposition, choose to respond with love and grace. Pray for those who criticize or discourage you, and trust that God will be your defender.

Surround Yourself with Supportive People: Seek out mentors, fellow believers, and friends who will encourage and uplift you. Positive relationships will help you stay motivated in the face of challenges.

"No weapon formed against you shall prosper, and every tongue which rises against you in judgment you shall condemn." (Isaiah 54:17, NKJV)

LACK OF RESOURCES

Challenge:

At times, a lack of financial resources, time, or skills can make fulfilling God's purpose feel impossible. You may struggle with feelings of inadequacy or wonder how you will accomplish what He has called you to do.

130

How to Overcome:

Trust God for Provision: God is the ultimate provider. He is more than capable of supplying your needs—whether financial, spiritual, or practical (Philippians 4:19).

Step Out in Faith with What You Have: Use what God has already given you. Be faithful with the small things, and trust that He will multiply your efforts as you walk in obedience.

Collaborate with Others: God often works through community. Partner with people who can contribute their time, talents, or resources to help fulfill His plans.

"And my God shall supply all your need according to His riches in glory by Christ Jesus." (Philippians 4:19, NKJV)

SPIRITUAL WEARINESS

Challenge:

Pursuing your purpose is a long-term commitment that requires endurance. At times, you may feel spiritually drained, discouraged, or weary—especially if progress seems slow or obstacles persist.

How to Overcome:

Find Rest in God: Prioritize physical and spiritual rest. Jesus invites us to come to Him for renewal and peace (Matthew 11:28).

Renew Your Mind: Strengthen yourself by meditating on God's promises and keeping an eternal perspective. His Word provides the encouragement and wisdom needed to push through difficult seasons.

Rely on His Strength: Your strength comes from God. When you feel weak, lean on Him—He will empower and sustain you (Isaiah 40:31).

"But those who wait on the Lord shall renew their strength; they shall mount up with wings like eagles, they shall run and not be weary, they shall walk and not faint." (Isaiah 40:31, NKJV)

Every challenge you face on the journey to fulfilling your God-given purpose is part of His refining process. Even in the difficulties, He is strengthening you, equipping you, and leading you closer to His plan. Keep your eyes fixed on Him, trust in His guidance, and take faithful steps forward. Through perseverance and reliance on God's strength, you will walk in the purpose He has set before you.

THE ROLE OF FAITH AND OBEDIENCE IN FULFILLING YOUR PURPOSE

Faith and obedience are foundational pillars in discovering and living out God's purpose for your life. Without these two elements, your purpose may remain unclear or unfulfilled. As a believer, you are called to trust in God's plan and walk in obedience to His will. Faith is the trust and confidence you place in God, while obedience is the action that follows your faith. Together, they guide you toward your God-given purpose.

1. Faith as the Foundation

Faith is the belief that God has a purpose for your life and that He will guide you in fulfilling it. Without faith, it is impossible to please God (Hebrews 11:6). Faith empowers you to trust in His promises, even when circumstances are uncertain or challenging. When you step out in faith, you declare your trust in God's goodness, His ability to direct your steps, and His faithfulness to complete the work He has begun in you.

How Faith Shapes Your Purpose:

Confidence in God's Plan: Faith assures you that God's plan for your life is good, even when your circumstances seem unclear. Trusting in His sovereignty allows you to follow His calling, even when it feels risky or uncomfortable. He knows the end from the beginning and promises to work all things together for your good (Romans 8:28).

Hope in God's Timing: Faith cultivates patience, helping you trust in God's perfect timing. The fulfillment of your purpose may take time, and delays can be discouraging. However, faith keeps you steadfast, knowing that God's timing is always right.

A Vision of the Unseen: Faith allows you to see beyond your current reality and embrace the purpose God has for you. As Hebrews 11:1 (NKJV) states, "Now faith is the substance of things hoped for, the evidence of things not seen." Even if you don't yet see the full picture, faith provides assurance that God's plan is unfolding.

"For we walk by faith, not by sight." (2 Corinthians 5:7, NKJV)

2. Obedience as the Action

Obedience is the tangible expression of faith. It's easy to say you believe in God's purpose, but true faith is demonstrated through action. Following God's commands and direction shows that your faith is genuine. Obedience is an act of trust in His wisdom and authority. Without obedience, faith remains passive, but when activated, it moves you closer to fulfilling God's purpose.

How Obedience Drives Purpose:

Aligning with God's Will: Obedience ensures that your life is aligned with God's will. By following His Word and promptings, you position yourself to walk in the path He has prepared for you. This alignment is crucial for fulfilling your purpose and staying on the right course.

Access to God's Blessings: Obedience unlocks God's blessings and favor. As Deuteronomy 28:2 (NKJV) promises, "And all these blessings shall come upon you and overtake you because you obey the voice of the Lord your

God." Walking in obedience allows you to experience the fullness of what God has for you.

Overcoming Distractions and Temptations: The world offers countless distractions that can pull you away from your calling. Obedience strengthens you to resist temptations and remain focused on God's purpose.

A Willing Heart: Obedience is not just about following rules—it's about having a willing heart to do what God asks, no matter how difficult it may seem. It requires stepping out in faith, even when the path is uncertain, trusting that God will provide what you need to fulfill your purpose.

"If you are willing and obedient, you shall eat the good of the land." (Isaiah 1:19, NKJV)

3. The Power of Faith and Obedience Working Together

Faith and obedience are not separate forces; they function as two sides of the same coin. Faith empowers you to trust in God's purpose, while obedience compels you to act on that trust. When combined, they create a powerful synergy that propels you forward in fulfilling God's calling.

Why Faith and Obedience Are Essential for Living Out Your Purpose

Faith Lays the Foundation, Obedience Builds the Structure: Faith is like the blueprint for your purpose, providing vision and direction, while obedience is the action that brings that vision to life. Without faith, there is no plan; without obedience, the plan remains unrealized.

Without Faith, Obedience Becomes Empty: If you obey God without fully trusting in His goodness and plan, your obedience can feel like mere obligation rather than a heartfelt response. But when obedience is rooted in faith, your actions become meaningful, purposeful, and fulfilling.

Without Obedience, Faith Remains Incomplete: "Faith without works is dead" (James 2:26). It is not enough to simply believe in God's purpose—you must actively live out that belief. Obedience is the tangible expression of faith, demonstrating trust in God's guidance and perfect timing.

"Faith by itself, if it does not have works, is dead." (James 2:17, NKJV)

LIVING OUT YOUR PURPOSE WITH FAITH AND OBEDIENCE

Faith and obedience are the keys to unlocking and fully living out God's purpose for your life. When you trust in His promises and respond with obedience, you step into the fullness of His calling. These two elements empower you to overcome doubts, challenges, and distractions, allowing you to walk confidently in your God-given purpose.

Throughout Scripture, we see how faith and obedience shaped the journeys of Abraham, Moses, and Jesus, paving the way for the fulfillment of God's plan. In the same way, as you continue your journey, trust that with God's help, you can do all things. He will guide you every step of the way.

A Prayer for Purpose

SAY THIS PRAYER:

"Heavenly Father, thank You for creating me with a purpose. I surrender my life to You and ask for Your guidance as I seek to fulfill the plans You have for me. Help me walk in obedience, reflect Your love, and bring glory to Your name. Strengthen me to overcome challenges and keep my focus on You. Use me, Lord, as a vessel for Your kingdom. In Jesus' name, Amen."

Reflection: How Can You Live Out God's Purpose Today?

Take a moment to reflect on your life and consider the following:

In what area do you feel called to make a difference?

How can you serve others in your community, workplace, or church?

What steps can you take today to align your life more closely with God's purpose?

What specific gifts or talents has God given you, and how can you use them for His glory?

Are there any fears, doubts, or distractions holding you back from living out your purpose?

What steps can you take this week to grow closer to God and align your life with His plan?

Write down your answers and bring them before God in prayer. Ask Him to reveal His will and empower you to walk boldly in your calling.

Living out God's purpose requires intentionality and action. Invite the Holy Spirit to show you specific ways you can be a light in the world and reflect God's glory. Then, step out in faith, knowing that every small act of obedience contributes to God's greater plan.

WALKING IN GOD'S PURPOSE

Living out God's purpose is the greatest adventure we can embark on. As we step into the good works He has prepared for us, we discover true fulfillment and joy. We are called to be lights in the world, reflecting His glory and drawing others to Him.

When we trust in God's ultimate plan—both for this life and for eternity—we can walk with hope and confidence. May we continue to embrace the purpose for which we were created, knowing that our lives are woven into His magnificent story.